THE ROAD
TO GREATNESS

追寻伟大

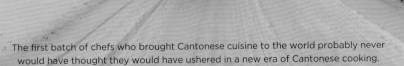

The first batch of chefs who brought Cantonese cuisine to the world probably never would have thought they would have ushered in a new era of Cantonese cooking.

Every great journey starts from a daring dream and is accomplished one step at a time. Born and bred in Guangzhou, Guangzhou Automobile Group Motor Company ("GAC Motor") has made a quantum leap from a Chinese auto brand to a world-class auto brand. GAC Motor has completed its decade of endeavor and progress with a pioneering, practical attitude that is characteristic of the Cantonese people.

第一批将粤菜滋味带向世界的大厨，可能从未想过一个崭新的时代就此开启。

伟大的征程，源于勇敢的梦想，成于一步步的行动。从中国汽车品牌到世界级汽车品牌，发端于广州的广汽传祺，以广东人特有的敢为人先和求真务实精神，走过了砥砺奋进的十年。

THERE WOULD BE NO REASON TO DREAM

Though young in the auto industry, GAC Motor is at the forefront among Chinese brands in development speed. It is a proprietary brand that has crystallized the best efforts of all employees at GAC Group – a Fortune Global 500 company.

Shortcuts are never an option for GAC Motor which is always taking on challenges head-on and with optimism. The company constantly challenges itself to be a pacesetter in the auto industry and always strives to be the equal of the best automakers in the world. Driven by dreams, unwavering in its commitment to the strategy of "high-end-focused, quality-first and innovation-driven", GAC Motor has built a sequence of medium and premium vehicles. With its matrix of high-end vehicle models – as represented by GA8 Sedan, GS8 SUV and GM8 Minivan – now in full swing, GAC Motor has become the first Chinese automaker with a complete rollout of luxury C-class vehicles.

梦想如果只是梦想
就没有存在的意义

作为风华正茂的中国汽车品牌，广汽传祺是世界 500 强企业——广汽集团举全力发展的自主品牌，发展速度居中国品牌前列。

不走捷径，以乐观态度直面未知和挑战，向最伟大的对手看齐，广汽传祺逐梦而上，坚守"定位高端、品质优先、创新驱动"的战略方针，一步步构建中国汽车工业中高端品牌的基因序列，以传祺 GA8、GS8、GM8 为代表的高端车型矩阵也让其成为首

GREATNESS IS IN THE DETAILS
AND IS MANIFESTED IN EVERY SINGLE STEP
IN THE RIGHT DIRECTION

For gourmets with a discerning palate, the freshness of ingredients, coupled with utmost attention to details in cooking, is what makes a great Cantonese dish.

GAC Motor always puts quality first and abides by international standards in vehicle development and production, never relenting in pursuing its overarching goal of alluring design, reliable components, reassuring manufacture and heartwarming services. To ensure quality in products and services, GAC Motor has built a full life-cycle quality management system with comprehensive detail control ranging from vehicle design to production processes, sales and after-sales services. Thanks to its commitment to quality, the company has managed to retain its position as the highest ranking Chinese brand in J.D. Power Asia Pacific's 2017 China Initial Quality Study (IQS) for the fifth consecutive year.

伟大，构筑于每一个细节
见证于每一天的进步

材料的新鲜，烹饪的用心，是一道好粤菜经得起挑剔的基础。

广汽传祺恪守品质，坚持国际标准造车，以动心的设计，放心的零件，安心的制造和暖心的服务的"四心"品质为终极原则，构铸出一整套全生命周期质量管控体系，从汽车设计、生产流程、销售以及售后服务全方位细节管控，为品质奠定坚实基础。在全球权威市场研究机构 J.D. Power 发布的 2017 年中国新车质量研究报告（IQS）中，传祺已在中国品牌中连续五年名列第一。

INNOVATION-DRIVEN PRODUCTION, FROM MADE-IN-CHINA TO DESIGNED-IN-CHINA

Thanks to its tradition of drawing strength and inspiration from other cuisines, Cantonese cuisine has developed 21 unique cooking techniques. The cuisine stays fresh and alive at all times through constant innovation.

GAC Motor is convinced that core technologies and original designs are always worth every effort and every penny of investment. After a decade of development, GAC has built a global R&D network to keep its core technologies in sync with the world's latest trends. As it stands today, GAC has established two North American R&D centers respectively located in Silicon Valley and Detroit, as well as an advanced design center in Los Angeles.

Looking to the future, GAC Motor will drive cross-sectoral innovation in the auto industry through cooperation with leading high-tech companies around the world, so as to help lay the foundation for the rise of auto ecosystems with smart driving at the core, smart transportation and smart cities.

创新驱动
从中国制造到中国"智"造

众采百家所长，不断创新，21种独特的烹饪手法让粤菜在时间的洪流里愈显生命力。

广汽传祺坚信：核心技术和原创设计永远是逐梦路上的源动力。十年潜心发展，广汽传祺跨越国界建成了全球研发网，真正让核心技术与世界保持同步。目前，广汽已在北美地区成立了硅谷研发中心、底特律研发中心，以及洛杉矶前瞻设计中心。

广汽传祺还与全球顶尖科技企业共同促进汽车行业的跨界创新，为未来以智能驾驶为核心的汽车生态圈、智慧交通、智慧城市奠定基础。

BE FEARLESS,
THE BRAVE ARE THE PIONEERS OF GREATNESS

Cantonese chefs are known for going with the flow of seasons and treating Mother Nature with awe and respect. With a reverence for Mother Nature and with the naturalness of ingredients as its soul, Cantonese cuisine has firmly established itself on the world's culinary map.

Likewise, GAC Motor is and has always been committed to building an automobile ecosystem featuring harmonious coexistence between humans and nature. The company regards energy saving, environmental protection, emission reduction, consumption cutbacks and cyclic utilization as the principles for developing a world-class plant that is green, environmentally-friendly and energy efficient. GAC Motor is the first-ever Chinese brand to have received a gold-level review from C-ECAP (China Eco-Car Assessment Program). In addition, GAC Motor is working closely with Sanjiangyuan ("Three-River-Source") National Park Administration and World Wildlife Fund (WWF) in building China's first national park. It also organizes periodic volunteer activities for protecting the ecology of Sanjiangyuan which contains the headwaters of three great rivers of China: the Yellow, the Yangzte and the Lancang. By so doing, the company is making good on its promise to help create a better future for humanity.

无惧重负，勇敢者面前才有路

对自然心存敬畏，遵循四季轮换；粤菜以选材天然为魂，尊重自然，立足世界。

广汽传祺致力于打造人与自然和谐共存的汽车生态，恪守节能、环保、减排、降耗、循环利用的原则，构建了绿色、节能、环保的世界级生态工厂，成为首个获得 C-ECAP 中国生态汽车评价金牌的中国品牌。此外，广汽传祺联手世界自然基金会 WWF、三江源国家公园管理局，共建中国首个国家公园，并定期开展志愿者行动，保护长江、黄河、澜沧江三大河流的发源地生态，只为人类更好的未来。

BUILDING A WORLD-CLASS BRAND AND A GLOBAL COMPANY

Though born and bred in Guangdong, Cantonese cuisine has flourished on the global food scene. The cuisine now enjoys a high status in the culinary world, which could not have come about without the dedication of enterprising Cantonese chefs who, generation after generation, have never stopped spreading their culinary footprint around the world.

The playing field of the world is never closed. Applause and acclaim go only to the extraordinary. As a rising star in the auto industry, GAC Motor has the courage to venture into the world's toughest and most challenging markets, whether emerging or mature. Today, GAC Motor has established its business presence in 15 countries across five major regions – the Middle East, Southeast Asia, East Europe, Africa and America, thus becoming the only Chinese auto brand to have successfully penetrated overseas markets with medium and high-end products.

GAC Motor is always committed to its mission of creating an enjoyable life of mobility for all. Looking to the future, GAC Motor will remain consistent in its dedication to pursue the ultimate with craftsman spirit and keep moving forward for the realization of its dream. GAC Motor believes if everyone dares to pursue greatness, the world would be a better place.

世界级品牌　全球化企业

源于广东，风靡全球，粤菜的世界化进程，与敢为人先的传承者密不可分。

世界的舞台，为勇者敞开。从新兴市场到成熟市场，广汽传祺都将自己置身于最具挑战的世界竞争环境中，目前已完成中东、东南亚、东欧、非洲、美洲五大板块 15 个国家的布局，成为唯一一个以中高端产品成功切入国际市场的中国汽车品牌。

广汽传祺始终以"创造愉悦的移动生活"作为自己的品牌使命。未来，在前往世界的征途中，广汽传祺仍将追求极致，逐梦前行，并坚信：如果每个人都敢于追寻伟大，世界将会更美好。

米其林指南
THE
MICHELIN
GUIDE

FINE CANTONESE FOOD
BY THE MICHELIN GUIDE
ASIA - EUROPE - USA

米其林指南粤菜
亚洲-欧洲-美国

2018·19

MICHELIN

DEAR READER,
亲爱的读者

Cantonese cuisine is one of the 'Four Great Traditions' of Chinese cooking. Founded in Lingnan, it is known for its precise techniques and large variety of ingredients, meticulous control of time and heat during cooking, and the diversity of its cooking methods. Cantonese cuisine can be further subdivided into Guangzhou, Chao Zhou, Hakkanese and Shunde cuisine, and the four types all have their unique features and strengths. Merging the strengths from these different provinces, Cantonese cuisine is both tempting and unforgettable, for local and travelling gourmets alike.

This year, the Michelin Guide is working in cooperation with GAC (the Guangzhou Automobile Group Motor Co.) to introduce this guide to top Cantonese cuisine. Cantonese really has become the leading representative for Chinese cuisine, and from Asian cities to Western countries, the footprints of Cantonese restaurants are spread around the globe. To track down the best restaurants from Asia, Europe and America, our team of professional inspectors scoured every region to conduct anonymous visits. The selection includes restaurants with our famous Michelin Stars ✿; our award for great value, the Bib Gourmand ⊛; and the Plate ⊪○, which represents a good meal.

Over two decades, the GAC Group has strived to bring Chinese automobiles to the rest of the globe - in the same manner that Cantonese dishes reached out to the world, allowing international gourmets to understand the time-honoured Chinese food culture. GAC's mission of "creating an enjoyable life of mobility" coincides with the Michelin's commitment to readers to make their travels safe and enjoyable. With this guide, we invite you to explore the many different Cantonese restaurants on your journeys and to experience the unique delicacies of Lingnan.

发源于岭南的粤菜是中国传统四大菜系之一，素以用料精细广博、着重火候、做法灵活善变等见称，兼具多个外省菜系之长，海纳百川而自成一家。若精细分类粤菜尚可分为广府菜、潮州菜、客家菜、顺德菜等几种地方风味，四系各具特色，各有所长，叫广东人念念不忘，饕客趋之若鹜。

粤菜餐馆在全球美食版图上无远弗届，堪称中国菜系的代表，亚洲各地城市固然踪影处处，欧美等地亦从未缺席。为让读者体验粤菜精粹，米其林指南今年特意伙拍踏入二十周年的广汽集团，推出这本以粤菜为题的指南。评审员踏遍全球，以匿名身份到访不同食店，网罗亚洲、欧洲及美国各地出色的粤菜馆，当中不乏素质特别出色的星级餐厅✿，也有价廉物美的必比登推介⊛和评审员万里挑一的米其林餐盘推介⊪○。

二十年来，广汽集团竭力让中国汽车走向全球，正如粤菜走出国际，让各地饕客洞悉中国久经历练的饮食文化。广汽"创造愉悦的移动生活"的宗旨，正与米其林指南对读者的承诺不谋而合。愿乘着这本小指南，大家能在旅途上尝尽齿颊留香的粤菜餐厅，体会岭南独特的绝顶滋味。

CONTENTS
目录

ASIA
亚洲

P. 30

EUROPE
欧洲

P. 272

USA
美国

P. 332

CANTONESE CUISINE,

A TASTEFUL CONSTELLATION

粤菜——
滋味荟萃

With thousands of years of glorious history, Chinese food culture is profound and refined in every sense. From ingredient selection to cooking techniques, every little detail is considered by chefs well-informed by centuries of accumulated experience and wisdom. Rare ingredients from the deepest oceans and the highest mountains transcend their own flavours in the chefs' skilful hands to form divine dishes which can impress even the most jaded gastronome. Various regional cuisines with their own unique characters make China the ultimate destination for foodies from around the world.

Among all of these Chinese cuisines, Cantonese is by far the most well-known outside of China. Cantonese restaurants around the world amaze food lovers across different cultural and ethnic backgrounds, making Cantonese the quintessential must-try for anyone who wants to experience the most captivating cuisine of Chinese food culture.

"" 中华饮食文化传承千年，从食材到烹调技艺无一不琢磨讲究，背后蕴含着的是久经历练的智慧与经验。大江南北的山珍海错经厨师巧手升华成令饕客回味再三的佳肴；中华各菜系百花齐放，其中粤菜堪称中国菜系的代表，粤菜餐馆踪迹遍及全球，为老饕趋之若鹜，是感受中华饮食魅力不可不尝的菜系。

CANTONESE FOOD: INSPIRED BY HISTORY AND TERROIR

Cantonese food is renowned and applauded for its exquisite tastes and exacting finesse. It originated from the Lingnan region in the south of the Nanling Mountains and later spread to Hong Kong, Macau, Southeast Asia, and then all over the world.

The long history of Cantonese cuisine is heavily influenced by the terroir – the mountains and sea in the province foster an abundant supply and a dazzling variety of the freshest ingredients that have inspired generations of talented chefs. Guangdong (formerly Canton) Province's early exposure to Western culture also made it a perfect place for exotic ingredients and foreign cooking to meet with traditional Chinese methods.

An eclectic mix of the West and the East gives Cantonese cuisine its unique character, earning its name as one of the top four Chinese cuisines in the late Qing Dynasty. According to different geographical locations within the province, Cantonese cooking is further divided into four sub-regional cuisines, namely Guangzhou, Chao Zhou, Hakkanese and Shunde, each with their unique cooking methods and taste profile.

盛载悠久历史的广州美食

粤菜,发源于岭南,流传至港澳乃至东南亚,立足全球。独特的风味饮誉四方,精湛技艺广受称颂。

悠长的历史促成了粤菜的形成——广州包山带海,各类新鲜食材应有尽有,得天独厚的地理环境使得广东地区厨师取材广泛,数千年前已有蛇馔出现;华洋杂处的历史亦令异国材料及烹饪技术于此交流融和,糅合各家,使广州菜式形成独成一帜的强烈风格,晚清时期已成为中国四大菜系之一。而在这菜系中,按地域又形成了风味各异的广府菜、潮州菜、客家菜及顺德菜几大流派。

NATURAL FLAVOURS

The heart and soul of Guangzhou cooking is freshness. The abundance of natural resources, due to its proximity to mountains and the sea, has spoiled and inspired Guangzhou chefs and diners with a smorgasbord of top quality ingredients. And in the case of a seafood dish, for example, the fish is expected to be alive just seconds before it is cooked, because freshness is key to flavour. As only the best ingredients are used, the chefs tend to just bring out their authentic tastes without over-seasoning. Despite the wide array of cooking methods involved, Guangzhou cooking emphasises natural umami flavour, which has become the delicate signature of this cuisine.

广府菜 烹出原味

粤菜四系当中,广府菜为标志性的代表;而广府菜的精粹,就是尝鲜。邻海依山,物产富饶令广府菜食材范围无远弗届,被宠坏的广东厨师与食客对食材的要求是必须新鲜,现宰现烹并讲究火候。由于选料精细,厨师们注重原汁原味地呈现食材,富变化的烹调方法,加上强调烹出自然鲜味的原则,造就了鲜美细腻的广府菜风味。

BARBECUE MEAT
OF INTERNATIONAL FAME

Cantonese cuisine also inevitably conjures up the image of luscious, succulent barbecued meats. Poultry and pork are marinated and chargrilled to perfection thanks to the chefs' exceptional skills. Be it char siu pork in honey glaze, roast goose or suckling pig, the skin is always crispy, while the meat is tender and juicy. Cantonese barbecued meat is now enjoyed by foodies all over the world and has become one of the representative foods for Cantonese cuisine.

广式烧味 扬名国际

若论广府菜，烧味也是不可或缺的一员：利用炭火的热力，配合厨师的纯熟手法，各式家禽或肉类经腌制并烤炙成叫人吮指的叉烧、烧鹅或乳猪，皮酥脆、肉嫩滑，其独特风味使之成为广东名物，也是粤菜走到国际的重要代表之一。

REGIONAL CANTONESE CUISINES

Along with Guangzhou cooking, the other three sub-regional Cantonese cuisines are not to be missed. The Hakka people migrated from the north to the south, so they needed to preserve food and to eat substantial meals in order survive the long journey and the physical hardship. Thus, Hakkanese cuisine is characterized by many salted ingredients and hearty dishes, such as salt-baked chicken and braised pork belly with salted mustard greens.

Chao Zhou has a long coastline and is famous for its seafood. Chao Zhou people have developed a range of unique ways to cook seafood, including serving it raw, frying it, braising it, marinating it in spiced soy and making seafood congee, seafood fritters or even seafood soups. Kung Fu tea, with its initially bitter and astringent taste that slowly turns into a lingering, almost sweet, bouquet, is the best way to cut through the richness of a Chao Zhou meal.

Another famed gourmet region, Shunde, bases its cuisine on Nanhai cooking and borrows influences from the counties surrounding it. Shunde people are serious about their ingredients and very specific about cooking steps. Famous dishes such as scrambled egg white with milk in Da Liang style, fried stuffed dace, and steamed whole pig Jun An style, present unique flavours and textures.

迁徙生活和体力劳动令客家人擅于以盐保存食物,故多以腌制食材入馔,也由此出现了客家咸鸡、梅菜扣肉等多油多咸菜式。

而海产较多的潮州,发展出独特的海鲜吃法,生吃、煎煮、煲粥、烙、腌、放汤,五花八门;吃罢海鲜和以盐和卤水等佐料调和的食品以后,更别忘了啜一杯先涩后甘的功夫茶解腻。

被评为美食之都的顺德,菜式以南海菜为基础,糅合数派菜式技巧而成,因为选料与烹制认真,造就了极具风味的大良炒鲜奶、煎酿鲮鱼、均安蒸猪等特色佳肴。

粤菜四系 精彩亮丽

广府菜以外,切莫忽略其他三系的独特魅力——客家人由北南徙作"客",

On top of maintaining traditions, Cantonese food constantly reinvents itself by blending influences from different culinary cultures. Over the years, talented chefs have been sourcing ingredients and seasonings from around the world, blending modern cooking techniques to conjure up novel Cantonese dishes that keep abreast of the times while pleasing the eyes and the palate. This is also what makes Cantonese cuisine shine bright on the global map of culinary art.

善于融汇贯通一直是粤菜强项,随着时日推演,厨师们更广泛地运用世界各国的食材、调味料及烹调方法来演化菜式,推陈出新,令人目不暇给,这也是粤菜能享誉国际、跻身全球美食舞台的真谛。

THE MICHELIN GUIDE'S COMMITMENTS

Whether they are in Japan, the USA, China or Europe, our inspectors apply the same criteria to judge the quality of each and every restaurant and hotel that they visit. The MICHELIN guide commands a **worldwide reputation** thanks to the commitments we make to our readers – and we reiterate these below:

Our inspectors make regular and **anonymous visits** to restaurants and hotels to gauge the quality of products and services offered to an ordinary customer. They settle their own bill and may then introduce themselves and ask for more information about the establishment.

To remain totally objective for our readers, the selection is made with complete **independence**. Entry into the guide is free. All decisions are discussed with the Editor and our highest awards are considered at an international level.

The guide offers a **selection** of the best restaurants and hotels in every category of comfort and price. This is only possible because all the inspectors rigorously apply the same methods.

All the practical information, classifications and awards are revised and updated every year to give the most **reliable information** possible.

In order to guarantee the **consistency** of our selection, our classification criteria are the same in every country covered by the MICHELIN guide. Each culture may have its own unique cuisine but **quality** remains the **universal principle** behind our selection.

Michelin's mission is to **aid your mobility**. Our sole aim is to make your journeys safe and pleasurable.

承诺

不论身处日本、美国、中国或欧洲，我们的独立评审员均使用一致的评选方法对餐厅和酒店作出评估。米其林指南在世界各地均享负盛名，关键在其秉承一贯宗旨，履行对读者的承诺：

评审员以匿名方式定期到访餐厅和酒店，以一般顾客的身份对餐厅和酒店的食品和服务素质作出评估。评审员自行结账后，在需要时会介绍自己，并会详细询问有关餐厅或酒店的资料。

为保证本指南以读者利益为依归，餐厅的评选完全是我们独立的决定。我们不会向收录在指南内的餐厅收取任何费用，所有评选经编辑和评审员一同讨论才作出决定，最高级别的评级以国际水平为标准。

本指南推介一系列优质餐厅和酒店，当中含括不同的舒适程度和价格，这全赖一众评审员使用一致且严谨的评选方法。

所有实用资讯、分类及评级都会每年修订和更新，务求为读者提供最可靠的资料。

为确保指南的一致性，每个国家地区均采用相同的评审和分类准则，纵然各地的饮食文化不同，我们评选时的准则完全取决于食物素质和厨师的厨艺。

米其林的目标多年来贯彻始终——致力令旅程尽善尽美，让您在旅游和外出用膳时不但安全，且充满乐趣。

STARS

Our famous One ✿, Two ✿✿ and Three ✿✿✿ Stars identify establishments serving the highest quality cuisine – taking into account the quality of ingredients, the mastery of techniques and flavours, the levels of creativity and, of course, consistency.

✿✿✿   Exceptional cuisine, worth a special journey!

✿✿   Excellent cuisine, worth a detour!

✿   High quality cooking, worth a stop!

BIB GOURMAND

This symbol indicates our inspectors' favourites for good value.

PLATE

Good cooking.
Fresh ingredients, capably prepared:
simply a good meal.

THE MICHELIN GUIDE'S SYMBOLS

         Interesting wine list

         Notable cocktail list

FACILITIES & SERVICES

         Great view

         Terrace dining

         Wheelchair access

         Air conditioning

         Private room

         Valet parking

         Car park

         Counter

         Reservation required

         Reservation not accepted

         Dim sum

         Restaurant offering vegetarian menus

         Cash only

米其林图标

供应优质餐酒

供应优质鸡尾酒

设施及服务

上佳景观

阳台用餐

轮椅通道

A/C 空调

私人厢房

代客泊车

P 停车场

柜台式

需订座

不设订座

点心

供应素食菜单

S 只接受现金

米其林美食评级分类

星级美食

闻名遐迩的米其林一星✽、二星✽✽和三星✽✽✽推介，推荐的是食物素质特别出色的餐厅。我们的评级考虑到以下因素：材料的素质和搭配、烹调技巧和味道层次、菜肴所展示的创意，少不了的是食物水平的一致性。

✽✽✽　卓越的烹调，值得专程造访。
✽✽　　烹调出色，不容错过！
✽　　　优质烹调，不妨一试！

必比登美食推介餐厅

必比登标志表示该餐厅提供具素质且经济实惠的美食。

米其林餐盘

评审员万里挑一的餐厅，食材新鲜、烹调用心，菜肴美味。

FoodCollection/Photononstop

ASIA
亚洲

GUANGZHOU
广州

BINGSHENG MANSION
炳胜公馆

The main dining room and the 32 private rooms exude an understated glamour. Championing innovative and refined Cantonese fare, it serves hand-crafted dim sum at lunch, such as sachima with olive nuts which is rarely seen these days. Special char siu uses pork belly that is marinated overnight and grilled till crispy. Other must-try items include stir-fried flat rice noodles with sliced beef, signature pineapple buns and roasted juicy goose.

对一般粤菜馆的烦嚣环境生厌？不妨到以欧陆风格设计、设三十多间厢房的炳胜公馆用膳。餐厅主营原味、新鲜的精品粤菜，主厨钟师傅定期研发新菜式，引以为傲的作品包括冷水猪肚、每天限量十五只的荔枝鸡，和肥而不腻的秘制黑叉烧等等。爱好一盅两件的客人不妨于早午市光临，可尝到价格亲民的创意点心，还有几近绝迹的手工茶点。

亚洲

GUANGZHOU
广州

TEL.+86 20 3803 5000
5F, Shoufu Mansion, 2 Xiancun Road, Zhujiang New Town, Tianhe
天河区珠江新城洗村路2号首府大厦5楼
www.bingsheng.com

BingSheng Mansion • southtownboy/iStock

BINGSHENG PRIVATE KITCHEN
炳胜私厨

GUANGZHOU
广州

TEL.+86 20 8757 5699
178 Tianhe East Road, Tianhe
天河区天河东路178号
www.bingsheng.com

The décor re-creates the old-time charm of luxury mansions in Xiguan district, while the art and cut flowers add a tasteful touch. The menu focuses on healthy cooking with seasonal organic ingredients. Double-boiled soups are made with mountain spring water. Signature dishes include fried Boston lobster with black pepper and chilli, braised gourd with female mud crab, and street-style stir-fried flat rice noodles with sliced beef. Reserve a table two or three days ahead.

餐厅以岭南元素作设计主题，着意营造出往昔西关大户的用餐感觉，缀以不同画像及鲜花，富有格调。菜式方面，注重挑选优质时令及绿色食材，特别是炖汤全用山泉水熬制。招牌菜有黑椒炒波士顿龙虾、斗门膏蟹炆黑毛节瓜、及东主也爱吃的街边炒河粉。集团每周均派专员试菜，新菜式也经东主员工品评才推出，确保水准。建议于两至三天前订座。

BingSheng Private Kitchen

✿

JADE RIVER
玉堂春暖

Diners unwind here with a cup of tea freshly brewed by tea masters. The traditional garden, water features, exquisite wood work and artisan Manchurian windows give it a serene feel. The food is, of course, no less impressive. Steamed sunflower seed-fed chicken is delivered straight from the farm daily. Baked pigeon with lemongrass and salt is another proud creation of the chefs. Also try various poultry and meat in white marinade.

餐厅设计带中国古风，岭南庭院的设计分隔开包厢及散座，深色刻木装潢，配以全木造家具，中式瓦顶上更挂着鸟笼，十分优雅；而室内的彩色满州窗更是历史悠久且已停产的手工玻璃，倍添古意。餐厅必试菜式有每天早上新鲜由百万葵园送到的白切葵花鸡，以及由两位大厨共同研制的香茅焗乳鸽，白卤水也不容错过。

GUANGZHOU
广州

TEL.+86 20 8188 6968

3F, White Swan Hotel, 1 Shamian South Street, Liwan
荔湾区沙面南街1号白天鹅宾馆3楼
www.whiteswanhotel.com

♿ ⇔ 🅿 🍽

Jade River

JIANG BY CHEF FEI

江

Its classic Cantonese fare prepared with a modern twist makes this restaurant one of the most popular among locals. Chef Fei bases his cooking on time-honoured traditions, but revolutionises them with touches of creativity. Try his versions of roasted goose and char siu pork – juicy meat enrobed in crispy skin and crust. Dim sum is nicely presented, especially the dessert that includes a deep-fried bird-shaped rice dumpling with coconut milk.

餐厅主厨辉师傅以其巧手为传统粤菜带来突破，把时令配料透过经典烹调手法创制成一道道崭新佳肴，令餐厅成为广受本地人欢迎的食店。在此用餐必定要尝尝皮脆肉嫩的烧鹅与叉烧，无可挑剔的精致点心同样令人一试难忘；各种粤菜的新滋味必会令食客有另一层次的用餐体验。

GUANGZHOU
广州

TEL.+86 20 3808 8885

4F, Mandarin Oriental Hotel, 389 Tianhe Road, Tianhe
天河区天河路389号文华东方酒店4楼

www.mandarinoriental.com/guangzhou

Jim Cheung Hin/Jiang by Chef Fei

LAI HEEN

丽轩

With years of experience, chef Guo believes wok qi matters most in Cantonese cooking. That's why he stir-fries in a small cast iron pan. He uses only the best ingredients and stock is made with chicken skinned, deboned and simmered in spring water for hours. Try his steamed sunflower seed-fed chicken; fish maw black garlic soup; and star grouper poached, steamed with egg white, and wok fried with celery and onions.

餐厅主厨经验丰富，对粤菜之精粹：镬气与鲜味极为注重，故所有小炒菜式均坚持以小平镬烹煮。食材方面亦相当新鲜及讲究，如烹鸡必选用以葵花籽饲养的葵花鸡，炖汤的鸡更会去皮去骨，加上用矿泉水烹煮，清澈味美。推介龙腾四海及过桥东星，四川风味的小炒亦不容错过。晚上光临更能欣赏到古筝演奏。

GUANGZHOU
广州

TEL.+86 20 3813 6688

3F, The Ritz-Carlton Hotel, 3 Xing An Road, Zhujiang New Town, Tianhe

天河区珠江新城兴安路3号富力丽思卡尔顿酒店3楼

www.ritzcarlton.com/guangzhou

ASIA 亚洲

LEI GARDEN (YUEXIU)
利苑（越秀）

It may be an outpost of the Hong Kong-based chain, but it is a household name among locals and tourists alike. The menu is similar to other branches, with the emphasis on traditional Cantonese fare, long-boiled soups and double-boiled soups. The chic dining room adorned with elegant chandeliers, beige textured walls and embroidery art, is always full. Regulars usually pre-order popular items when booking a table, such as crispy roasted pork belly.

秉持此香港集团特色，菜单除了提供一系列传统粤菜，驰名的老火汤及炖汤亦无缺席；冰烧三层肉等拿手菜式更令本地及外地人慕名而至。总是坐无虚席的餐室装潢走传统风格，悬起优雅的吊灯，以刺绣图案点缀淡色墙身，盛载鲜活海产的鱼缸更为中餐馆的布置画龙点睛。想尽享招牌菜建议于订座时先作预留，以免扑空。

ASIA 亚洲

GUANGZHOU
广州

TEL.+86 20 8363 3268

4F, Yi An Plaza, 33 Jianshe Sixth Road, Yuexiu

越秀区建设六马路33号宜安广场4楼

WISCA (HAIZHU)
惠食佳（海珠）

The kitchen crew has been here for a long time and they follow ancient recipes passed down through generations for their quality Cantonese food that is very reasonably priced. Apart from the sizzling swamp eels in claypots (known as Che-che eels), the restaurant is famous for healthy soups that are double-boiled for over four hours. The mantis shrimps are fleshy and bursting with sweetness. Reservations are recommended.

餐厅由小店起家，所以在价钱及口味方面依然亲民；同样保持的是其一贯水准的味道，有赖多为老员工的大厨及厨房团队秉持古法制作、用料新鲜，将传统风味代代相传。店内以啫啫系列闻名，每天炖煮四小时以上的广东炖汤亦是必尝，啫啫黄鳝煲则深受客人爱戴。餐室設多个包厢，建议提前预订。

GUANGZHOU
广州

TEL.+86 20 3438 1188
172 Binjiang West Road, Haizhu
海珠区滨江西路172号
www.shnoble.com/wisca

ASIA 亚洲

Wisca

YU YUE HEEN

愉粤轩

Helmed by Chef Mai with over 30 years of experience, this restaurant serves exquisite Cantonese dishes. Every course embodies the utmost finesse and detail-oriented approach the chef insists on. The signature pan-fried minced shrimp stuffed sliced lotus roots with crab meat looks effortless, but captures the heart and soul of Cantonese cooking in its entirety. The expansive view and the chic and very comfortable ambience is also a plus.

立足於四季酒店，愉粤轩为饕客烹调出至为精美的粤菜。有逾三十年丰富经验的主厨在厨房中掌控每一个细节，务求以巧手烹制出最顶尖菜式。黑松露百花煎酿藕夹是他其中一道招牌菜，简单中见功夫，呈现出粤菜之精粹。餐厅居高七十一层，用餐时有广袤的城市景观相伴，更显高雅气派。

GUANGZHOU
广州

TEL.+86 20 8883 3371

71F, Four Seasons Hotel, 5 Zhujiang West Road, Zhujiang New Town, Tianhe

天河区珠江新城珠江西路5号四季酒店71楼

www.fourseasons.com/guangzhou

Yu Yue Heen

CHUANG FA
创发

Despite its many tables on two levels, reservations are recommended here as it is always jam-packed with diners. The menu is traditional Cantonese with a highlight being the nourishing double-boiled soups. 'Real-taste' chicken (with the free-range option for extra) and fried pork large intestines with basil leaves are the big hits not to be missed. Seafood lovers should also check out the live fish tank at the entrance.

开业多年，供应传统而价格相宜粤菜的创发深受广州食客欢迎。谈及粤菜少不了老火汤，而餐厅的滋补炖汤便是其招牌菜之一，此外还有真味鸡，设有价格较高的走地鸡供客人选择；紫苏爆大肠也十分受欢迎。喜好海鲜的话店内也有提供新鲜海产。餐厅楼高两层，二楼设厢房，但经常座无虚席，建议先行订座。

GUANGZHOU
广州

TEL.+86 20 8188 1915
512-2 Guangfu North Road, Liwan
荔湾区光复北路512-2号

DAYANG (WENMING ROAD)
达扬原味炖品（文明路）

GUANGZHOU
广州

160-1 Wenming Road, Yuexiu
越秀区文明路160-1

Among locals, its name is synonymous with double-boiled soups which dominate the menu. Apart from the top-selling silkie chicken soup in whole coconut, other popular soups such as free-range chicken soup with goji berries and yam, and quail soup are trickier to order as they are rotated on a three-hour cycle. That means you never quite know what exactly is available in advance. Adventurous eaters may also try the turtle jelly with milk and honey.

这家炖品专门店在文明路上几乎无人不晓，每隔两至三小时，就有一盘盘炖品自厨房端出，店外人龙不绝，全因其炖汤以用料足、汤清甜驰名，其中尤以原盅椰子炖竹丝鸡最受欢迎。炖品出炉时间不定，要吃到特定类型炖品要靠点运气。炖品之外，佐以牛奶及蜂蜜的龟苓膏也是热捧之品。

Michelin

FAMOUS CUISINE
半岛名轩

The founder of the group is a restaurant magnate who's been in the business for over forty years and is a local celebrity. His mission is to promote no-frills Cantonese cuisine and he insists on using only the freshest ingredients. There are two menus – a standard one for all branches and one for specialities available exclusively at this branch. Must-try items include roasted beef rib and stir-fried sea whelk, lily bulbs and celery in XO sauce.

餐厅创办人从事饮食行业四十多年，经验老到，从细心安排菜单上已可见一斑。除了所有分店的统一餐单外，更于不同分店特设主厨拿手菜菜单，以切合不同顾客之口味。而每道菜式均坚持以新鲜食材烹制，贯彻粤菜朴实鲜活的味道，同时亦希望将营养和快乐带给客人。此店的招牌菜是生烧牛肋骨以及XO酱西芹百合炒螺片。

GUANGZHOU
广州

TEL.+86 20 8755 5928

2-3F, China Mayors Plaza, 189 Tianhe North Road, Tianhe

天河区天河北路189号中国市长大厦2-3楼

www.hl-bandao.com

 ♿ ⇩ **P** ◐❚❙

Michelin

NAN YUAN
南园

Dining rooms are adorned with colourful Manchurian windows that frame the landscaped garden views nicely. The menu features Cantonese cuisine and also some Chao Zhou cooking. As most diners are from the neighbourhood, the owner puts more emphasis on the food than service. Note that the charge depends on the grade of the room you dine in. If you want more comfort and privacy, and are willing to pay more, talk to the front desk.

GUANGZHOU
广州

TEL.+86 20 8444 8380
142 Qianjin Road, Haizhu
海珠区前进路142号

偌大的空间划分成不同区域，以斑斓的满州窗作点缀，令環境生色不少，且将园林美景尽收眼底。菜单上提供粤菜和特色潮州菜，切合本地人的口味。由於服务对象主要为附近街坊，店内注重食物的品质胜於一切；餐厅内的房间分设等级，若想有较为舒适的用餐环境可向前台服务员查询，但消费则会略高。

WAN HIN
云轩

This is the place to sample a variety of Chinese cuisines under one roof, including Cantonese, Sichuanese, Chao Zhou and Fujian, all made by chefs from the respective regions. The décor is traditionally Chinese, with abstract ink paintings in the hallways, works of famous Zhanjiang painters in the private rooms, and retro furniture, carved wooden windows and brick walls adorning the main dining room.

位於云来斯堡酒店，云轩共占三层，设二十四间厢房；设计洋溢中国气息，除了房内挂了湛江名画家的作品外，三楼的大厅设计也别出心裁，砖墙和木雕窗花加上中式怀旧桌子，带出浓厚东方味道。店内供应粤菜、川菜、潮州菜和福建菜等不同菜系的中式料理，且各由来自该地区的厨师主理。

GUANGZHOU
广州

TEL.+86 20 3868 3011

3-5F, Vanburgh Hotel, 126 Huangpu West Avenue, Tianhe
天河区黄埔大道西126号云来斯堡酒店3-5楼

www.vanburgh.com

XIANG QUN
(LONGJIN EAST ROAD)
向群（龙津东路）

Enduringly loved by locals for over 20 years, this started out as an 'ice parlour' serving cold drinks and light meals. These days the menu features no-frills home-style fare, including the signature steamed Qingyuan chicken, spring onion chicken, soy-marinated goose and baked fried fish head. The made-to-order swamp eel claypot rice boasts a crispy crust and an oniony aroma. Seafood lovers should ask about the catch of the day.

历久不衰的家的味道，让这饭店开业逾二十年仍深受食客喜爱。店子实而不华，菜式价廉物美。售卖的家乡菜中以选用清远鸡的白切鸡及葱油鸡最为有名，其他招牌菜还有豉油碌鹅及煎焗大鱼头。而其香气四溢的即制黄鳝饭更是不容错过。喜好尝鲜的话也可向店员查询菜单外的海鲜菜式。

GUANGZHOU
广州

TEL.+86 20 8188 5146

853-857 Longjin East Road, Liwan
荔湾区龙津东路853-857号

⇔ ◎ 🖫

XIN TAI LE (HAIZHU)
新泰乐（海珠）

This is not just a restaurant, but a gastronomical institution known for its signature eel dishes. Though this three-storey branch is not the original shop, it has been serving the neighbourhood for over two decades. Swamp eel rice is cooked in eel soup and topped with eel juices and oil. Swamp eel casserole boasts chunks of fresh eel that are springy and tender, coated in a Chu Hou-based sauce. Their fatty charsiu pork is also worth trying.

深具广州风味的老字号餐馆自有其独特魅力，而此店远近驰名的黄鳝菜式更是令人难以抗拒。虽非旗下总店，但开业近二十年足证其烹调素质千锤百炼，以柱侯酱作基础的巧手黄鳝煲，选用新鲜鳝块，肉质爽嫩；黄鳝饭则以鳝骨熬制之鳝汤煮饭，并拌上以鳝汁及鳝油混合而成的鳝酱，真材实料。占地三层的餐室附有贵宾房，适合大伙儿聚餐。

GUANGZHOU
广州

TEL.+86 20 8440 0711

2-4F, 93-99 Jiangnan West Road, Haizhu

海珠区江南西路93-99号2-4楼

⊞ 🅿 📞🍴 ⑤

ASIA 亚洲

Michelin

XIN TAI LE (YUEXIU)
新泰乐（越秀）

A household name known for its signature swamp eel rice, the chain came from humble beginnings, having started life as a street stall over 30 years ago. Of all the branches, this one in the old part of town retains the authentic atmosphere of its precursor most faithfully. Without fancy décor, this casual and bustling place, open till 3 am, makes a great spot for late-night drinks while enjoying the eels.

这家前身为大牌档、名为泰乐菜馆的餐厅已在老城区经营超过三十载，其黄鳝饭远近驰名。易名为新泰乐后，室内装潢保留着昔日的大牌档风味，纵然殷勤的服务和华丽的装饰皆欠奉，但一道道巧手黄鳝菜式、能与亲友们举杯畅饮的气氛足以弥补。顾及一众喜爱夜宵的客人，餐厅更营业至凌晨三时。

GUANGZHOU
广州

TEL.+86 20 8354 5431

Sino Trade Centre, 63 Panfu Road, Yuexiu
越秀区盘福路63号华茂大厦

Michelin

🙂

ZE 8
啫八

Despite the Song Dynasty-inspired décor and faux-antique stoneware, this place feels young and trendy. On its menu are about 30 dishes served in sizzling claypots complemented by an array of home-made sauces. Out of respect for Cantonese classics, the owner avoids food combinations that are overly fancy. The claypots with wider bottoms are tailor-made in Guangxi province to have more contact area so preventing the food from burning.

打破煲仔饭予人土气之感，餐厅走时尚年青路线，东主致力保留粤菜风味，提供多达二、三十款的啫啫煲，备有多款秘制酱汁，亦特别于广西订制底部接触面大的煲具，避免餸菜煮焦，并经常更换以确保效果。店内环境采用宋朝风格，别有古意，半开放式厨房透出的熊熊镬气及吱吱声响更堪称视听享受。

GUANGZHOU
广州

TEL.+86 20 3438 2088
174 Binjiang West Road, Haizhu
海珠区滨江西路174号
www.shnoble.com/ze8

🅿 ⇄ ⓞ🍴

ZHU ZAI JI SHI FU
(JIANGNAN AVENUE)
朱仔记食府（江南大道）

A hawker-stall-turned restaurant now with two branches – this three-storey casual joint with a bustling atmosphere is prized for its authentic Cantonese food, especially the juicy and flavoursome roast geese, a big hit among diners for the past 20 years. Other specialities include giant river fish shipped straight from Xijiang every day; salted pork trotters; Zhu Ji steamed chicken; and blackened barbecue pork.

由老字号大牌档慢慢发展成现时的酒家，装潢仍是走大众化路线，楼高三层的餐室甚是宽敞明亮。二十多年来以烹制地道粤菜闻名，自然讲究食材新鲜度及品质，其中鱼类特选西江特大河鲜，每天由专车运到。推荐菜式为朱记白切鸡、马来黑叉烧和金牌咸猪手等，古法烧鹅皇更是赫赫有名。设逾十间厢房，是各式聚会的上佳选择。

GUANGZHOU
广州

TEL.+86 20 8423 8356
429 Jiangnan Avenue South, Haizhu
海珠区江南大道南429号

Michelin

BEIYUAN CUISINE
北园

A rare gem at the heart of the busy city centre – it faithfully re-enacts the delicate details of a Lingnan-style Chinese garden, including a pair of stone lions. The interior is equally impressive, showcasing 14 gilded redwood vases with elaborate carvings on all sides. Opened in 1928, it is famed not only for its palatial décor, but also its seemingly simple Cantonese home-style dishes that are impeccably made.

屹立八十多年的北园酒家像世外桃园般：不论城市如何瞬息万变，仍是一片隔绝繁嚣的园林景色。红灯笼高挂，石狮子坐镇，配上斑烂的满洲窗，古意盎然亦甚有气派。菜式方面有各式各样的巧手粤菜，厨师将各类菜肴处理妥当，难怪不论商家、文人雅士或是大小家庭均爱於此处细味回味无穷的一餐。

GUANGZHOU
广州

TEL.+86 20 8356 3365
202 Xiaobei Road, Yuexiu
越秀区小北路202号
www.beiyuancuisine.com

ASIA 亚秀

GUANGZHOU
广州

TEL.+86 20 3428 6910

33 Dongxiao Road, Haizhu
海珠区东晓路33号

www.bingsheng.com

BINGSHENG PIN WEI (DONGXIAO ROAD)
炳胜品味（东晓路）

The group first made its name with sashimi and, at this branch, diners may choose from sea perch, grass carp, amberjack and a myriad of live prawns. It also prides itself highly on the unmissable 'four beauties' on the menu. Crispy barbecued pork is pork belly crusted in breadcrumbs and sugar before grilling. Pork trotters are braised in Japanese soy and maltose for hours. Cold pork tripe and goose intestine with soy sauce are also good.

楼高三层，设有宴会厅及五十间包厢，但最精彩亮丽的仍是餐厅内的一品粤菜。时令菜式推陈出新，而必点招牌菜有脆皮叉烧、冷水猪肚、豉油皇鹅肠及和味猪手，每款均是选料精细，且经长时间细心烹调而成；同样享负盛名的是女店东亲自引入的炳胜鱼生，依循顺德食法，佐以配料品尝。配合店内的环境及服务，想细味南粤特色的话必须一试。

BingSheng Pin Wei

🍴

DONG XING (TIANHE)
东兴（天河）

Born to a family of chefs, the owner opened her first shop in Enping circa 1985. Famed for her rustic peasant-style cooking, she opened this branch in 2005 and has another one in Panyu. The signature swamp eel rice in claypot uses only live wild-caught eels delivered on the day, deboned and shredded. Customers also come for creamy taro with taro sprouts in claypot and traditional braised goose. Reservations recommended.

女东主兼主厨來自厨师世家，但最初经营的餐厅业务未如理想，于是想出特色菜黄鳝饭，并不断改良至成为招牌菜。黄鳝饭食材每天现购，必选野生中型黄鳝且拆骨处理。其他食材亦每天由恩平总店直送。此店独家菜肴包括古法炆鹅及鲫鱼锅靭菜汤，还有农家芋苗煲，采用恩平独有芋苗和山区的香芋，菜式滑溜馥香，具浓厚农家菜风味。宜先行预约。

GUANGZHOU
广州

TEL.+86 20 3882 4101

1F, Hanfeng International Hotel, 6-8 Tianhe North Road, Tianhe
天河区天河北路6-8号汉风国际大酒店1楼

ASIA
亚洲

DR. XU'S WELLBEING BRANCH
徐博馆岭南养生菜

GUANGZHOU
广州

TEL.+86 20 3807 8889

7F, Zhonghe Plaza, 57 Linjiang Avenue, Zhujiang New Town, Tianhe
天河区珠江新城临江大道57号中和广场7楼

www.nanhaiyucun.com

The founder Dr Xu is a registered Chinese herbalist who advocates therapeutic diets. This restaurant doubles as a museum showcasing his antique collection and rare medicinal herbs. The Cantonese believe in the tonic effects of double-boiled soups and there is a vast array on the menu. Most dishes combine seasonal ingredients with natural health-boosters. Also ask the friendly team about the live seafood available.

有注册中医师资格的创办人将养生、健康饮食的理念贯彻融合于餐饮之中。为了推广保健文化，店内菜式除重视选材时令与否外，更配合不同保健食材及烹调法，务求令客人享受美食之余同时养生；菜单设计上有不少炖汤选择。此外，店内亦提供不少生猛海鲜，客人可向殷勤的服务员查询。环境俨如其名，如博物馆般陈设了不少东主的收藏品供客人品味。

Michelin

E GONG CUN (LIWAN)

鹅公村（荔湾）

Geese from the restaurant's own farm feature heavily on the menu. The must-try E Gong soup is a healthy herbal tonic made only with 120-day-old male geese – and you can smell its herbal aroma the moment you walk into the restaurant. Goose is cooked in a variety of ways – roasted, marinated, braised or simmered. The dining rooms are located in glass-clad houses that surround a pond.

名字已點出餐厅的食品主题：各式各样以鹅为主的佳肴，例如明炉烧鹅、卤水鹅及各種炆煮菜式，但最著名的要数其鹅公汤，选材严谨，取用120日以上的公鹅，連同多种中药材经细心熬制，味道温和、香气更是充溢餐室。鹅公村拥有自己的生态养殖场，保证品质。餐厅环境优美，中央有天鹅湖，两旁有玻璃屋供举办小型聚会。

GUANGZHOU
广州

TEL.+86 20 8151 3428
402-404 Haudi Avenue South, Liwan
荔湾区花地大道南402-404号
www.arloy.com

⇔ 🅿 ◎‖

ASIA
亚洲

Michelin

FIVE ZEN5ES
中国元素

Here you can experience the many facets of authentic Cantonese cuisine. Try their signature dishes such as boiled beef ribs with baked sea cucumber and onion oil, or stir-fried shrimps and noodles with chilli sauce. Apart from Cantonese, other regional specialities are also on offer. The modern and relaxing environment, contemporary décor and refined atmosphere, coupled with attentive service, makes for a pleasant experience.

一流氛围之下，此餐厅着意透过真正新式的烹调手法，为客人呈现粤菜层出不穷的顶级味道。必试菜有味汁牛肋排及干煸脆虾球和辣酱面。如果你爱好在摩登、舒适的环境中，享受细心的服务员为你送上一道道地道特色美食，此处将会是你的好选择。

GUANGZHOU
广州

TEL.+86 20 8918 1226

2F, Westin Pazhou, Area C, Canton Fair Complex, 681 Fengpu Middle Road, Haizhu

海珠区凤浦中路681号广交会展馆C区威斯汀酒店2楼

www.westin.com/pazhou

ASIA 亚洲

Five Zen5es

GUANGZHOU RESTAURANT (WENCHANG SOUTH ROAD)

广州酒家（文昌南路）

Since 1935, this four-storey restaurant on the main drag in Liwan district has been serving classic Cantonese cooking. As you enter, you can't miss the banyan tree at the centre of the building – it's the same age as the restaurant itself. Tea and cover charges vary depending on seating zones. The annexed store sells preserved meat and snacks to take home, such as palmiers and pineapple cakes.

楼高三层的餐厅位处行人如鲫的上下九路，竖立于餐厅中央、树龄逾八十年并陪伴着餐厅成长的老榕树是其一大特色。客人除了可选择能欣赏树景的普通茶市座位，亦可选择茶芥收费较高但较舒适安静的位置，第四层更设包厅，可主动向店员查询。餐厅旁兼营手信店，售卖各式腊味和蝴蝶酥、凤梨酥等小吃。

GUANGZHOU
广州

TEL.+86 20 8138 0388
2 Wenchang South Road, Liwan
荔湾区文昌南路2号
www.gzr.com.cn

🍴

HAI MEN YU ZI DIAN (YANLING ROAD)

海门鱼仔店（燕岭路）

GUANGZHOU
广州

TEL.+86 20 3720 5609

Jinyan Mansion, 120 Yanling Road, Tianhe

天河区燕岭路120号金燕大厦

♿ **P** ◑🍴

The dining room sports a high ceiling, faux-industrial pendant lamps, a hardwood floor and chic furniture amidst stylised Chinese motifs. It's essentially an up-market hawker stall experience in an air-conditioned space. It doesn't have a menu – instead, diners pick their food at the entrance where seafood is laid out neatly on ice. Staff will also tell you the other specialities available that day, such as soups, marinated meats or chilled crabs.

在舒适的室内环境中享用大牌档风味的机会不多，这店子就满足了这个愿望。餐厅设计西化，工业风吊灯配以木桌皮椅，恰配店家标榜的高级大牌档概念。店内不设菜单，是由客人到门口位置亲自挑选，或由服务员介绍合意的海鲜後再由厨师按客人自选的方式烹调；另外也有一些预先煮好的菜式，诸如蚬、蟹等海鲜和潮州卤味、汤品等供选择。

Hai Men Yu Zi Dian

HAI YAN LOU (BINJIANG EAST ROAD)
海晏楼（滨江东路）

The two chefs once worked at a prestigious hotel and their skills are unquestionable – which is why it's so hard to get a table here. Try their 'premium trio' which were usually only served at state banquets – rich and buttery foie gras, plum-scented squabs with crispy skin, and springy goose webs and wings in white marinade. Barbecue meat is grilled daily in limited servings. Arrive early to avoid disappointment.

由两位曾於知名宾馆主理国宴的主厨坐镇，水准自然具保证，故店内总是座无虚席。两位主厨各司其职，分别主理驰名烧鹅卤水及煎炸煮炸。招牌菜有至尊三宝，当中的法国鹅肝质感软润，味道浓郁；外皮爽脆的梅子乳鸽亦是一绝。卤水用上廿多年的秘方及特制器具，保有传统风味；烧味每天现烧且限量供应，想尝试的话也许要早点出行。

GUANGZHOU
广州

TEL.+86 20 3430 5888

2F, Jiangpan Huating, 1040 Binjiang East Road, Haizhu
海珠区滨江东路1040号江畔华庭2楼

ASIA 亚洲

HE YUAN (TIANHE)
和苑（天河）

The two-storey building houses a palatial dining room where rustic no-frills Cantonese fare is served. It opened in 2009 before relocating to this location in 2017. Top-notch ingredients are handled meticulously. Be it dim sum, stir-fry, casserole or stew, every item is impeccably executed and the flavours always hit the spot. Thoughtful and friendly service adds to the overall experience.

於2017年迁至现址，札根广州近十年的和苑继续於富丽堂皇的宴会厅内为顾客提供朴实的广东菜。烹调用心，由食材用料起已是精挑细选，着重新鲜且处理恰当。制作上无论是点心或小菜，都将食材味道表现得宜。服务态度亲切殷勤，是筹办宴席的绝佳场所。整店楼高两层，可办多於二十桌的宴席，同时亦适合各大小团体包厢。

GUANGZHOU
广州

TEL.+86 20 8306 3668

Level 3 & 3M, IMP, 68 Huacheng Avenue, Tianhe

天河区花城大道68号IMP环球都会广场3及3M层

Michelin

IMPERIAL TREASURE FINE CHINESE CUISINE

御宝轩

This branch of the Singapore-based chain sports a dining room that is cosy rather than large; there are also private rooms. The chefs use quality local ingredients and tweak the recipes to suit the local palate. Signature dishes include crispy chicken stuffed with glutinous rice that needs to be pre-ordered one day ahead. Fried Sri Lankan crab with black peppercorns, and steamed river eel in Shaoxing wine are also worth trying. Reservations are a must.

照顾当地人口味并细心挑选食材设计菜式，也许就是餐厅成功的其中一个要素。来自新加坡的御宝轩可算是其中佼佼者，选料精细，即使是鸡的菜式，也会就烹调方法不同而用数款不同品种的鸡只配合，尽善尽美。招牌菜为需早一日预订的御宝金牌糯米炸子鸡及现点黑胡椒炒斯里兰卡蟹；女儿红蒸河鳗及手功菜荔芋香酥鸭亦不应错过。建议订座。

GUANGZHOU

广州

TEL.+86 20 3885 6382

L5-14B, IGC Mall, 222 Xingmin Road, Tianhe
天河区兴民路222号天汇广场
L5-14B

www.imperialtreasure.com

Imperial Treasure Fine Chinese Cuisine

GUANGZHOU
广州

TEL.+86 20 8567 1163

506 Linjiang Avenue East, Tianhe

天河区临江大道东506号

LIUHE CHA JU
六合茶居

There are nine Mongolian tents by the river along with the private rooms in the three-storey building. Those tents certainly make a meal here more fun. Traditional Chao Zhou fare is served here and the signature dishes include cold red swimmer crabs, marinated goose heads, and sliced marinated goose with Puning dried tofu. It only uses geese aged between 3 and 5 years from farms in Chenghai to ensure consistent quality.

楼高三层的餐厅内约有三十多间房，空间感十足；户外包厢的造形则仿如蒙古包，临近江边用餐，别具风味。餐厅对于食材同样重视，比如制作卤鹅头必选用养殖三至五年的澄海鹅以确保素质。招牌菜冻大红蟹或普宁豆干拼鹅肉也不容错过。喜爱品茗的客人不妨到门外的柜台查看售卖的茶叶及茶壶。

PANXI
泮溪

With over 70 years of history, it boasts a manicured garden and views of the lake and river, as if lifted out of an ancient painting. Daily Chinese music performances add to the total experience. The food is equally enchanting: the famous Macao-style roast pork uses only pork belly with five alternate layers of fat and meat for crispy skin and juicy flesh. Stuffed dace Shunde's style and winter melon soup with mixed seafood are unmissable.

欲于如古代般的清幽环境中用餐？开业七十年的泮溪或可满足願望。林景簇拥、尽收湖、河景色，加上特设诸如每天举办粤剧演奏等各种不同主题之厅房，古雅十足。店内佳肴不枉美景，驰名澳门烧肉用料讲究，必以脂肉相间的五层肉烹调，成品外皮鬆脆；家乡酿鲮鱼以及限量供应的八宝冬瓜盅同样不容错过。若想享用露天茶座，需留意只於早茶时段开放。

GUANGZHOU
广州

TEL.+86 20 8172 1328
151 Longjin West Road, Liwan
荔湾区龙津西路151号

ASIA 亚洲

PEACH BLOSSOM
桃园馆

Those familiar with the classic novel 'Romance of the Three Kingdoms' should be able to tell what inspired the name here. The interior is also heavily decorated with portraits of the protagonists and scenes from the 'Oath of the Peach Garden' episode. The food is home-style Cantonese cooking with seasonal specialities, and everything is made from scratch in-house; try the famous barbecue meat and dim sum. Private rooms are available.

熟悉三国演义的客人或可领略餐厅名称的典故由来；倘若未能意会也可从入口的结义亭及墙上多幅三国人物画像中猜到布置主题。餐廳专营粤菜及家常菜，部份时节更会推出时令菜式；所有食品不假外求，为团队的自家出品，而烧味及点心均是餐厅招牌菜。倘欲享有较私密的用餐环境，可以选择以三国人物命名的厢房。

GUANGZHOU
广州

TEL.+86 20 8333 8989

3F, LN Garden Hotel, 368 Huanshi
East Road, Yuexiu
越秀区环市东路368号花园酒店3楼
www.gardenhotel.com

Kong Weijun/Peach Blossom

SKY NO.1
空中1号

Perched on the edge of a river, this family-friendly restaurant caters to different party sizes and has several private rooms. It is known not just for its panoramic vista, but also for the quality of its food and service. Diners come to indulge in well-honed Cantonese cuisine and seafood while soaking in the views from the top floors of the skyscraper. The ink paintings dotting the dining room are also worth checking out. Reservations recommended.

临江而立，优秀的食物及服务素质令餐厅营业十年至今一直深受大众爱戴。位处廿八层楼高，可饱览到包含广州塔在内的灿烂夜景；餐厅环境不逊景色，除了大大小小的包厢让客人可在高私密度的环境下尽情用餐，更有不少鉴赏价值极高的水墨画。餐单上罗列各式粤菜和生猛海鲜，适合一家老幼共聚天伦。建议预早订座。

GUANGZHOU
广州

TEL.+86 20 3785 7111
28-31F, Xinhe Building, 1 Huaxia Road, Zhujiang New Town, Tianhe
天河区珠江新城华夏路1号信合大厦28-31楼
www.nanhaiyucun.com

Michelin

SUI XUAN
随轩

Brace yourself for the grandeur of this modern restaurant – the eight-metre high ceiling and the sheer expanse of space is quite amazing. The menu is classic Cantonese, made with seasonal ingredients. Try Chef Deng's crispy chicken, roast baby pigeon, and boiled yellow croaker with prawn and ginger; they all hit the spot with their tantalizing tastes and impeccable execution.

位处希尔顿酒店五楼，这家餐厅为客人提供正宗传统的粤式风味。甫进门，八米高的天花以及整个广阔现代的餐室已然令人赞叹。餐厅烹调出时令且地道的粤菜，主厨的拿手菜有脆皮鸡及烤乳鸽等，丰富的味道必会令你一试难忘。

GUANGZHOU
广州

TEL.+86 20 6683 9999

5F, Hilton Tianhe Hotel, 215 Linhe West Cross Road, Tianhe

天河区林和西横路215号天河希尔顿酒店5楼

www.guangzhou.tianhe.hilton.com

Shell.Young[ANGLE.PDJ/Sui Xuan

¶⃝

SUMMER PALACE
夏宫

The majestic red and gold colour scheme and opulent décor have become the unmistakable signature look of the restaurant and its namesakes in this international hotel chain. Chef Chan reinvents Cantonese classics with a refined touch. Try his juicy and tender charsiu pork, or his Peking duck with crispy skin in a glossy dark caramel colour. The views of the park are another highlight that adds to the dining experience.

主厨以精准的厨艺触觉烹调出精美的粤菜佳肴；在整个以标志性红、金色为主调的餐室中，品尝着厨房精研的传统粤菜，用餐体验极尽豪华高贵。必试菜式有不少人慕名而至的烧味：肉质松软且肉汁丰富的叉烧，烤至色泽乌亮的片皮鸭等。用餐时有园境相伴，更是赏心乐事。

GUANGZHOU
广州

TEL.+86 20 8917 6498

2F, Shangri-La Hotel, 1 Hui Zhan East Road, Haizhu

海珠区会展东路1号香格里拉大酒店2楼

www.shangri-la.com/guangzhou

✈ ㄥ ♻ ♨ 🅿 🍴

ASIA
亚洲

GZ ATUphoto Co., LTD./Summer Palace

TAO RAN XUAN (LIWAN)
陶然轩（荔湾）

The Chinese décor on the inside and European architecture on the outside can be confusing. But authentic Cantonese food has been served in this oxymoronic establishment, alongside the owner's antique collection and live Chinese zither performance, for several years. The food is equally memorable – its signature fish head casserole is rich with velvety cartilage. Pre-order the suckling duck in Kunming style as it tends to sell out.

GUANGZHOU
广州

TEL.+86 20 8120 2828
50 Shamian South Street, Liwan
荔湾区沙面南街50号

地道粤菜只能在装潢传统的餐馆中找到？这家开业七年的欧陆式建筑餐厅证明于优雅餐室中也可一尝如假包换的粤菜风味。室内放置东主的珍藏古董，室外则毗邻江边及公园，加上现场古筝演奏，氛围高雅之至，难怪不时有婚宴举办。食物亦毫不逊色，特色风味鱼头煲味道浓厚且鱼云鲜嫩，而手剪昆明乳鸭更是屡屡售罄的招牌菜，不想扑空建议先作预订。

Michelin

XIN HAO WEN

新浩文

To the regulars frequenting the restaurant since its opening in 2005, this feels like a second home and the friendly owner and waiting staff are like family. What the three-storey shop may lack in ambiance, it more than makes up in authentic street-style Cantonese food, such as deep-fried Bombay duck, paper-wrapped spare ribs, steamed chicken and sizzling fish tripe. It opens till late, so perfect for a round of drinks and some tasty bites.

满室老街坊令这经营传统粤菜的餐厅满载人情味。经多次搬迁后於2005年坐落於现址,共三层并設两个独立廂房。令老主顾一再光臨的秘诀除了是东主与员工的热情,也许还因为店内供应大量价钱相宜的地道菜式。招牌菜有必点的秘制纸包骨、秘制九肚鱼及和味豬手等,三五好友若想找寻好地方夜宵畅聚、把酒倾谈,不妨光临此处。

GUANGZHOU
广州

TEL.+86 20 8184 9738
84 Shanmulan Road, Liwan
荔湾区杉木栏路84号

GUANGZHOU
广州

TEL.+86 20 3769 1234

**68F, Park Hyatt Hotel, 16 Huaxia
Road, Zhujiang New Town, Tianhe**

天河区珠江新城华夏路16号柏悦
酒店68楼

guangzhou.park.hyatt.com

≪ ⇔ **P** ⓞⅢ

YUE JING XUAN
悦景轩

Diners get to see the chefs in action in the open
kitchen and the experience is quite something
– the flames, the aromas and more importantly,
the dynamic energy of the team. The chef has
17 years of experience in Cantonese cooking
and his sand ginger chicken is famed for its
tender and thick flesh – he uses only 225-day
old free-range chicken from Zhanjiang. Must-
try items also include crispy roast pork belly
and honey-glazed sleeper goby.

以家为概念的悦景轩采取开放式厨房设计,殷勤
的厨师团队就在身旁烹调,自是目不暇给;空气中
飘荡着食材的馥郁香气,更令人食指大动。在厨房
领军的主厨有十七年烹调粤菜经验,巧手名菜不
少,其中湛江沙姜鸡采用养殖225天的走地鸡烹
制,鸡肉丰厚,甚为驰名;此外,冰烧三层肉和作头
盘的蜜汁笋殼鱼亦不容错过。

Yue Jing Xuan

YUN PAVILION
韵轩

The lavish interior adorned with exquisite pieces is inspired by the eight categories of Chinese musical instruments, while the Longquan celadon teacups add a touch of class. Passionate about Cantonese food, Chef Tan insists on cooking only what's in season and finds ways to bring out their best flavours. Only 160-day-old chicken are used in his signature chicken dishes like rock salt baked chicken. Also try fried glutinous rice and sweetened almond cream.

诚如其名，餐室的设计布置极富中国古代色彩韵味，大至摆设，小至特别订制的龙泉青瓷，处处展露出设计师的心思。相得益彰的是厨师对中菜的热爱；钻研粤菜多年仍未止步，积极研究新菜式，务求保留传统之余带来冲击及新鲜感。食材方面要求严谨，坚持使用上乘时令食材。招牌菜有客家咸鸡、生炒糯米饭，新创制的青花葱油鸡也值得一试。

GUANGZHOU
广州

TEL.+86 20 3705 6585

5F, Conrad Hotel, 222 Xingmin Road, Zhujiang New Town, Tianhe

天河区珠江新城兴民路222号康莱德酒店5楼

www.conradhotels3.hilton.com

ASIA 亚洲

Michael Shiu/Yun Pavilion

HONG KONG
香港

✿ ✿ ✿

LUNG KING HEEN
龙景轩

Your first and only challenge will be attempting to secure a reservation at this most popular of restaurants. Chef Chan Yan Tak is one of Hong Kong's most experienced and respected chefs and every one of his dishes is as delicately crafted as it is tantalizingly presented. The name means 'view of the dragon' and the large room offers great views of the harbour but your attention will rarely wander from the stunning Cantonese food in front of you.

要在此家极受欢迎的餐厅用餐，最大最难的挑战是订座！经验充足、深受业内人士敬重的行政总厨陈恩德师傅掌管厨房命脉，他处理的菜式，每一道都是精致诱人的艺术品。偌大的空间，典雅时尚的布置，配上无敌维港海景，令人心旷神怡。然而，优美的环境从不曾将你的专注力从精美的食物上移离。

HONG KONG
香港

TEL.+852 3196 8880

4F, Four Seasons Hotel, 8 Finance Street, Central

中环金融街8号四季酒店4楼

www.fourseasons.com/hongkong/dining/restaurants/lung_king_heen/

✿ ⪝ ☆ ♿ 🍽 P ◖🍴

ASIA
亚洲

HONG KONG
香港

TEL.+852 2132 7898

1F, The Langham Hotel, 8 Peking Road, Tsim Sha Tsui

尖沙咀北京道8号朗廷酒店1楼

www.langhamhotels.com/hongkong

&♿ ♧ ♨ 🅿 🕪

❀ ❀ ❀

T'ANG COURT
唐阁

Sautéed prawns with asparagus, deep-fried taro puffs with shrimps, and lobster with spring onions are just some of the delicate and refined Cantonese classics you can expect at this discreet and professionally run restaurant. It comes divided into two: upstairs has a more subdued, intimate feel, while the traditional style of the more appealing first floor room is broken up by contemporary artwork; tables 23 & 25 are best.

以中国史上最强盛的唐朝命名，呈献各种粤式珍馐佳肴，露皇金银虾、荔芋宝盒、三葱爆龙虾等，光听名字已垂涎不已。这格调典雅的餐厅共占两层，一楼融合传统装潢与现代艺术装饰，23及25号台位置最佳；二楼较私密，适合情侣用餐或商务聚会，并设有以唐代诗人命名的贵宾厅。服务专业称心。

T'ang Court

FORUM
富临饭店

Everyone knows the name of Yeung Koon Yat, the owner chef of Forum; indeed, his signature dish of Ah Yat abalone has rapidly acquired iconic status and some have even been known to travel to Hong Kong from overseas just to try his delicacy. The new premises are more comfortable and contemporary than the old address and thankfully all the kitchen team made the move too. As well as abalone, you can try other options like pan-fried star garoupa.

各位对餐厅东主杨贯一的大名一定不会陌生。多年来不论是本地食客或世界知名人士，全是他的座上客，其招牌菜阿一鲍鱼更是天下闻名。此店搬至现址后，面积更广、装潢更豪华兼具时代感。满有默契的幕后团队聚首一堂为食客炮制美食。日本干鲍制作的砂锅鲍鱼和海鲜类如生煎东星斑等均不可错过。

HONG KONG
香港

TEL.+852 2869 8282

1F, Sino Plaza, 255-257 Gloucester Road, Causeway Bay
铜锣湾告士打道255-257号信和广场1楼

ASIA 亚洲

noel jones/Forum

SHANG PALACE
香宫

Lobster prepared in 35 different ways is just one of the specialities here at this sumptuously decorated room at the Shangri-La hotel. The kitchen is overseen by the experienced chef, and his longstanding brigade prepares the traditional Cantonese cuisine with considerable skill and obvious pride. Equal care goes into the charming and thoughtful service. The pretty room is decorated with a mix of antique Chinese window frames and Sung-style paintings.

35种龙虾烹调方式是香宫一大特色，华丽的室内布置是另一特色。由富经验主厨领军的厨房团队，以久经历练的烹调造诣，每道传统菜式均是细致与自信的结晶。体贴细心的服务同样叫人喜悦。古中国窗框与宋代风格油画，陈设漂亮的餐室变得更有韵味。

HONG KONG
香港

TEL.+852 2733 8754

Lower level, Kowloon Shangri-La Hotel, 64 Mody Road, East Tsim Sha Tsui

尖东么地道64号九龙香格里拉酒店地库1楼

www.shangri-la.com/kowloon

Shang Palace

🌸 🌸

SUN TUNG LOK (TSIM SHA TSUI)
新同乐（尖沙咀）

After 40 years in Happy Valley, Sun Tung Lok is now comfortably ensconced on the fourth floor of the Miramar shopping centre. A contemporary colour palette of grey, brown and beige is used to good effect in this stylish restaurant; ask for one of the three booths for extra privacy. The majority of the menu is Cantonese and dishes include rib of beef with house gravy, stuffed crab shell, and roast suckling pig; the abalone is a must.

在跑马地驻扎四十年后，新同乐现在于美丽华商场四楼继续营业。充满时代感的灰色、咖啡色与米色的巧妙配搭让店子看起来较摩登。店内设有三个厢座，以满足需要私人空间的客人。八成菜式是粤菜，包括烧汁干焗牛肋骨、鲜蘑菇焗酿蟹盖及烧乳猪件。这里的鲍鱼是必试之选。

HONG KONG
香港

TEL.+852 2152 1417

4D, 4F Miramar Shopping Centre, 132 Nathan Road, Tsim Sha Tsui
尖沙咀弥敦道132号美丽华商场
4楼D

www.suntunglok.com.hk

⇄ ©📶

ASIA
亚洲

❀❀

TIN LUNG HEEN
天龙轩

'Dragon in the sky' is a very apposite name as this good looking Cantonese restaurant occupies a large part of the 102nd floor of the Ritz-Carlton hotel. The vast windows bring in plenty of daylight at lunch and make it a good spot from which to watch the sun go down. Among the signature dishes are barbecued Iberian pork with honey, and double-boiled chicken soup with fish maw in coconut. There are also several charming private rooms.

位于丽思卡尔顿酒店102楼，这间极具气派的粤菜餐馆以气势十足的天龙命名。楼高两层的设计令餐厅光线充沛，格外舒适，殷勤的服务人员让你倍感亲切，另设有多个精致的私人包厢。菜单着重传统菜式，值得一试的有蜜烧西班牙黑豚肉叉烧和原个椰皇花胶炖鸡。

HONG KONG
香港

TEL.+852 2263 2150

102F, The Ritz Carlton Hotel, 1 Austin Road West, Tsim Sha Tsui
尖沙咀柯士甸道西1号丽思卡尔顿酒店102楼
www.ritzcarlton.com/en/hotels/china/hong-kong/dining/tin-lung-heen

🕸 ⬤ ⬤ ⬤ ⬤ 🅿 ⬤

Tin Lung Heen

YAN TOH HEEN

欣图轩

Its location in the InterContinental hotel may be somewhat concealed but it's well worth seeking out this elegant Cantonese restaurant and that's not just because of the lovely views of Hong Kong Island. The authentic, carefully prepared specialities include stuffed crab shell with crabmeat; wagyu beef with green peppers, mushrooms and garlic; double-boiled fish maw and sea whelk; and wok-fried lobster with crab roe and milk.

这家优雅的粤菜酒家就在洲际酒店大堂低座，所处位置可能较为隐蔽，但十分值得去寻找，而这里的魅力，绝不止于能够观赏香港岛的美景，更因其供应多款精心炮制的传统粤式佳肴，包括：脆酿鲜蟹盖、蒜片青尖椒爆和牛、花胶响螺炖汤及龙皇炒鲜奶等。

HONG KONG
香港

TEL.+852 2313 2243
InterContinental Hotel, 18 Salisbury Road, Tsim Sha Tsui
尖沙咀梳士巴利道18号洲际酒店
www.hongkong-ic.intercontinental.com

ASIA 亚洲

Yan Toh Heen

AH YAT HARBOUR VIEW (TSIM SHA TSUI)
阿一海景饭店（尖沙咀）

A large photo of chef-owner Yeung Koon Yat greets you as you come out of the lift – and he's enjoying his most famous dish: abalone. Ah Yat signature fried rice and stewed oxtail with homemade sauce and red wine casserole is also worth a try. The good value set lunch menu is a great way of experiencing many more of their Cantonese specialities. The contemporary dining room takes full advantage of the wonderful views; Table 11 is the best.

身处位于iSquare 29楼的阿一海景，当然要一尝主厨老板杨贯一的名菜：阿一鲍鱼。此外，不妨试试其他驰名菜如一哥招牌砂窝炒饭及红酒酱炆牛尾。饭店供应来自波尔多、加州、新西兰和澳洲的高级红酒。店内设有四间私人厢房，大部分座位都能欣赏宜人的维港两岸美景，11号餐桌景观最佳。

HONG KONG
香港

TEL.+852 2328 0983

29F, iSquare, 63 Nathan Road, Tsim Sha Tsui
尖沙咀弥敦道63号iSquare29楼

ASIA 亚洲

Ah Yat Harbour View

CELEBRITY CUISINE
名人坊

Having just six tables and a host of regulars makes booking ahead vital at this very discreet and colourful restaurant concealed within the Lan Kwai Fong hotel. The Cantonese menu may be quite short but there are usually plenty of specials; highlights of the delicate, sophisticated cuisine include whole superior abalone in oyster sauce; baked chicken with Shaoxing wine and, one of the chef's own creations, 'bird's nest in chicken wing'.

这家隐藏于兰桂坊酒店内的餐厅，看似不甚出众但别具魅力，地方虽小却常客众多，故此必须提早预约。这里的广东菜餐牌颇为精简，但全是大厨富哥的特选菜式，精美菜肴推介包括富哥顶级鲍鱼、花雕焗飞天鸡及自创菜式燕窝酿凤翼。

HONG KONG
香港

TEL.+852 3650 0066

1F, Lan Kwai Fong Hotel, 3 Kau U Fong, Central
中环九如坊3号兰桂坊酒店1楼

DUDDELL'S
都爹利会馆

HONG KONG
香港

TEL.+852 2525 9191

Level 3, Shanghai Tang Mansion, 1 Duddell Street, Central
中环都爹利街1号上海滩3楼
www.duddells.co

Not many restaurants come with their own 'Art Manager' but then Duddell's has always been about more than just serving food and hosts regular art exhibitions and screenings. The upstairs bar is a cool spot for a pre-dinner drink, while the restaurant itself is a stylish and contemporary space. In contrast to the surroundings, the Cantonese menu keeps things fairly traditional, with ingredients very much from the luxury end of the scale.

都爹利会馆是少数设有艺术项目经理的餐馆,除了专营传统粤菜,餐馆会定期举行艺术展览、电影欣赏和艺术沙龙等活动。阁楼酒吧宜于餐前歇息浅酌。主餐室布置时尚且风格独特,餐牌上所见均是传统菜式,选用的是高级矜贵食材。

Duddell's

FU HO (TSIM SHA TSUI)
富豪（尖沙咀）

Thanks to its authentic cooking, diners have been coming to this Cantonese restaurant on a hidden floor of the Miramar shopping centre for over a decade. Among the specialities that appeal to these scores of regulars are the signature abalone dishes, the bird's nest with almond cream and the fried rice 'Ah Yung'. The most recent refurbishment gave this comfortable and relaxing restaurant a contemporary and elegant look.

这家粤菜酒家凭着正宗的烹调方式打响名堂，即使位于美丽华商场不太起眼的一层，十多年来依然吸引无数饕客。招牌菜有阿翁鲍鱼、杏汁官燕、阿翁炒饭。布置时尚优雅，予人舒适悠闲感觉。

HONG KONG
香港

TEL.+852 2736 2228

Shop 402, 4F, FooLoft, Mira Place One, 132 Nathan Road, Tsim Sha Tsui

尖沙咀弥敦道132号
美丽华广场一期食四方4楼402号铺

Fu Ho

IMPERIAL TREASURE FINE CHINESE CUISINE
御宝轩

Finding success in Singapore and Shanghai, Imperial Treasure opened its first Hong Kong branch in the sky-scraping landmark, with panoramic views of the harbour. The stylish dining room is embellished with subtle Chinese touches, such as the ceramic Koi carps and calligraphy. A fish tank in the kitchen ensures live seafood is available every day. Poached garoupa in fish soup with crispy rice and stuffed crab shell are worth a try.

继新加坡、上海后，御宝饮食集团终于落户香港。选址在九龙半岛地标北京道1号，坐拥无敌维港两岸景色，加上时尚中带点中国风的设计——水泥墙上的3D陶瓷鲤鱼和梁柱上的书法——令人悠然神往！厨房内附设有鱼缸，每天都有鲜活的海鲜供应，脆米海鲜浸东星、糯米酿脆皮乳猪及法式蟹盖是招牌菜。

HONG KONG
香港

TEL.+852 2613 9800

10F, One Peking, 1 Peking Road, Tsim Sha Tsui

尖沙咀北京道1号10楼

www.imperialtreasure.com

ASIA 亚洲

Imperial Treasure Fine Chinese Cuisine

KAM'S ROAST GOOSE
甘牌烧鹅

The Kam family name is synonymous with their famous roast goose restaurant. This little place is owned by the third generation of the family and he wisely hired his father's former chef to ensure the goose is as crisp and succulent as ever. There's also suckling pig, goose neck and head, and goose blood pudding available. With only 30 seats, don't be surprised to see a queue.

从祖父辈创业至今历七十多年，甘氏出品的烧鹅早已远近驰名，现由第三代传人在湾仔开设全新餐馆，承传父辈厨艺。与父辈共事多年的老师傅以甘氏家传秘方炮制的烧鹅，挂在窗前令人垂涎欲滴。烧乳猪、鹅头和鹅红也非常美味。小店仅有三十个座位，故常见轮位或买外卖的人龙。

HONG KONG
香港

TEL.+852 2520 1110
226 Hennessy Road, Wan Chai
湾仔轩尼诗道226号
www.krg.com.hk

✗⁵⁵ ⑤

ASIA 亚洲

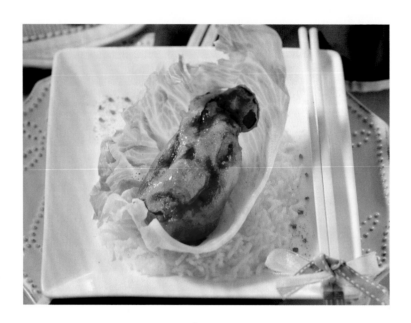

LEI GARDEN (KWUN TONG)
利苑酒家（观塘）

HONG KONG
香港

TEL.+852 2365 3238

L5-8, Level 5, apm, Millennium City 5, 418 Kwun Tong Road, Kwun Tong
观塘观塘道418号创纪之城第5期 apm5楼L5-8
www.leigarden.com.hk

Avoid the escalators and use the shuttle lift to get to the fifth floor in this confusingly arranged shopping mall. Once there, the set up will seem familiar if you've experienced other Lei Garden branches: dishes are standard Cantonese but are reliably cooked using fresh ingredients. The place is as frantic as the others but has been partitioned into different seating areas by smart trellises. Try not to sit near the entrance as it's noisy.

如欲更易找到和更快到达此酒家，请直接乘搭升降机到五楼。如你曾光顾其他利苑分店，对此店绝不会感到陌生：清一色的广东菜与可靠的美食及新鲜的材料。当然，这里同样挤满利苑的忠实顾客，简洁的屏风巧妙地将餐厅分隔成不同用餐区。

Lei Garden

LEI GARDEN (MONG KOK)
利苑酒家（旺角）

This is the original Lei Garden, which opened back in the 1970s; it's still as busy as ever so it's always worth booking ahead. The contemporary restaurant is spread over two floors and the upper space has views out onto the busy street. The long and varied Cantonese menu certainly represents good value; recommendations include tonic soups like double-boiled teal with Cordyceps militaris and fish maw.

由于这家餐厅实在太受欢迎，食客必须预先订座。此店是利苑总店，开业于七十年代。富时代感的餐厅共分为两层，楼上可看到旺角繁华的街景。以广东菜为主的菜单花样多变令人目不暇给，绝对物有所值。特别推荐各式炖品如蛹虫草须炖花胶水鸭。

HONG KONG
香港

TEL.+852 2392 5184
121 Sai Yee Street, Mong Kok
旺角洗衣街121号
www.leigarden.com.hk

ASIA 亚洲

Lei Garden

LEI GARDEN (NORTH POINT)
利苑酒家（北角）

Discreetly tucked away on the first floor of a residential block and overlooking a pleasant courtyard garden is this branch of the popular chain. Things here can certainly get quite frenetic as it accommodates up to 200 people. The lengthy Cantonese menu mirrors what's available at other branches, but particular dishes worth noting here are crispy roasted baby duck, deep-fried lotus root with minced pork and the daily seafood specialities.

这家深受欢迎的连锁酒家分店，隐藏在住宅大厦一楼。从酒家外望是屋苑的翠绿庭园，宽敞的空间可容纳多达二百人，气氛往往极为热闹。这里的菜单与其他利苑分店大致相同，特别推荐沙溪烧米鸭、家乡荔芋煎藕饼及每日海鲜精选。

HONG KONG
香港

TEL.+852 2806 0008

1F, Block 9-10, City Garden, North Point

北角城市花园9-10座1楼

www.leigarden.com.hk

ASIA 亚洲

Michelin

LOAF ON
六福菜馆

Spread over three floors and hidden behind a strip of seafood restaurants in Sai Kung is this neat little spot. The daily soup depends on what the owner buys from local fishermen; you can even bring your own fish and have it prepared by the kitchen. Besides seafood, Loaf On also offers simple but flavoursome Cantonese dishes like chilli and garlic bean curd, Loaf On-style chicken, and steamed sea fish with salt.

这家占了三层楼的小菜馆，藏身于西贡海鲜餐厅一带后街。店主每天从本地渔民处搜购最新鲜的食材炮制是日鱼汤，你亦可自行携带海鲜，交由厨师为你烹调。除了海鲜和鱼汤，椒盐奇脆豆腐和盐蒸海鱼也必须一试，别忘了预订一客风沙鸡。

HONG KONG
香港

TEL.+852 2792 9966
49 See Cheung Street, Sai Kung
西贡市场街49号

ASIA
亚洲

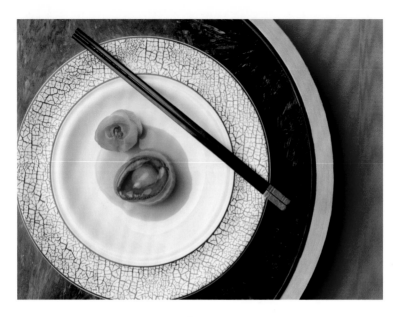

HONG KONG
香港

TEL.+852 2825 4003

25F, Mandarin Oriental Hotel, 5 Connaught Road Central, Central
中环干诺道中5号文华东方酒店
25楼

www.mandarinoriental.com/ hongkong/fine-dining/

MAN WAH
文华厅

Ceiling lamps resembling birdcages; original, ornate silk paintings; and local rosewood combine to create the striking interior of this Cantonese restaurant on the 25th floor of the Mandarin Oriental hotel. Tsui Yin Ting is their private room for 14 people and is styled on an old Chinese pavilion. The chef's specialities include steamed garoupa with crispy ginger and crabmeat, and roast goose puff with yanmin sauce.

位于文华东方酒店25楼的文华厅装潢华丽典雅，一盏盏仿鸟笼中式吊灯、墙上古色古香的丝绸画与紫檀木的运用带来了雅致的古中国情调。装饰一如中国古时凉亭的厢房聚贤亭能容纳十四人。酥姜珊瑚蒸星斑球及仁稔烧鹅酥皆为这儿的招牌菜。

Man Wah

MING COURT
明阁

There are two distinct dining areas in this elegant Cantonese restaurant on the 6th floor of the Cordis hotel: if you want a cosy, more intimate setting ask for Ming Sum, with its collection of Ming Dynasty bronzes; if you're coming in a larger group go for Ming Moon. Drunken sea prawns with Shao Xing wine, and roasted crispy chicken are among the specialities. The impressive wine list includes suggested pairings for your barbecued meat or abalone.

位于康得思六楼、装潢典雅的明阁分为两个截然不同的餐室：摆设着青铜器、充满古风的明日适合小型聚餐，大型聚会则可选择装潢较现代时髦的明月。此店提供多种餐酒，侍应还会协助顾客挑选适当佳酿配合菜肴佐吃。其招牌菜太白醉翁虾、明阁炸子鸡不容错过。

HONG KONG
香港

TEL.+852 3552 3028

6F, Cordis Hotel, 555 Shanghai Street, Mong Kok

旺角上海街555号康得思酒店6楼

www.cordishotels.com/en/hong-kong

ASIA 亚洲

Ming Court

PANG'S KITCHEN
彭庆记

Anyone living in Happy Valley will be familiar with Pang's Kitchen as it has been packing them in since it opened back in 2001. Its reputation is largely down to its Cantonese cuisine which comes in a decidedly traditional and homely style, with dishes such as baked fish intestines in a clay pot, whole superior abalone in oyster sauce, and seasonal dishes like snake soup. It is not a huge place so it's worth booking ahead.

跑马地的街坊必定不会对彭庆记感到陌生，店铺自2001年开业以来一直服务该区。其驰名粤式佳肴主要是家常小菜和传统菜式，如砵仔焗鱼肠、蚝皇原只吉品鲍及季节性菜式如太史五蛇羹。由于食店面积不大，食客宜预先订座。

HONG KONG
香港

TEL.+852 2838 5462
25 Yik Yam Street, Happy Valley
跑马地奕荫街25号

SPRING MOON
嘉麟楼

Oriental rugs, sepia prints of colonial life, teak floors and art deco styled stained glass all summon the spirit of a 1920s Shanghainese dining room here at The Peninsula hotel. Specialities are bird's nest soup, wok-fried lobster, and roasted Peking duck. The tea bar offers over 25 regularly-changing teas and staff, many of whom are sent to China for training, are hugely knowledgeable and happy to make recommendations.

餐室设计以半岛酒店开业时的二十年代老上海为蓝本,古典风格的柚木地板,配衬东方地毯、殖民地时代旧相片和带装饰艺术风格的彩色玻璃,充满怀旧气息。餐单上全是深受欢迎的经典菜式,包括千丝官燕羹、北京片皮鸭等等。店内提供的二十五种茶定期更换,曾到中国受训的侍应乐于回答茗茶知识。

HONG KONG
香港

TEL.+852 2696 6760
1F, The Peninsula Hotel, Salisbury Road, Tsim Sha Tsui
尖沙咀梳士巴利道半岛酒店1楼
www.hongkong.peninsula.com/zh/fine-dining/spring-moon-chinese-rest

SUMMER PALACE
夏宮

There's a timeless, exotic feel to this room whose decoration of gilt screens, golden silk wall coverings and lattice panels is inspired by the palace in Beijing. The menu is a roll-call of Cantonese classics; double-boiled soups are a speciality; dim sum is a highlight; and signature dishes include marinated pig's trotters, braised '23-head' Yoshihama abalone in oyster sauce, and Peking duck. They also offer a good selection of teas.

高耸的餐室以北京故宫为设计灵感,以华丽的水晶吊灯、大红色餐桌,配以传统中国屏风、金色丝绸画作及雕塑,营造了迷人的情调。菜谱罗列各款传统广东名菜,招牌菜包括沙姜猪脚仔、蚝皇吉品鲍鱼、北京片皮鸭等,炖汤也是其专长,部分需提早预订。午市时点心是不俗的选择。可供选择的茶饮也很多。

HONG KONG
香港

TEL.+852 2820 8552

5F, Island Shangri-La Hotel, Pacific Place, Supreme Court Road, Admiralty
金钟法院道太古广场港岛香格里拉酒店5楼

www.shangri-la.com/island

YAT LOK
一乐烧鹅

If you're after delicious roast goose then Yat Lok may fit the bill. This family business has been going since 1957 but moved to its current location in 2011. The owner-chef prepares his roast meats using a secret family recipe; his chicken in soy sauce and rose wine is well worth ordering. The place is basic and space limited – you'll be sharing your table with others – but the owner's wife and her team create a pleasant atmosphere.

一乐早于1957年开始营业，其后在2011年迁至现址。每次经过其门前，总会被挂在窗前的烧鹅吸引而垂涎三尺。以家族秘方腌制、经过二十多道工序炮制而成的烧鹅，色香味俱佳，蛮受街坊欢迎，其他食物如玫瑰油鸡也做得不错。

HONG KONG
香港

TEL.+852 2524 3882
34-38 Stanley Street, Central
中环士丹利街34-38号

ASIA 亚洲

YAT TUNG HEEN (JORDAN)
逸东轩（佐敦）

One to be filed under 'hidden gems', this Cantonese restaurant makes the best of its hotel basement location through warm tones and soft lighting. The kitchen keeps things traditional in order to highlight the natural flavours of the season's produce. Regulars love the roasted meats and double-boiled soups but other signature dishes include fried chicken with ginger and mandarin peel, and double-boiled pig's lung with fish maw in almond soup.

位处酒店地库的逸东轩在2017年进行全面装修。自1990年开业至今，一直为食客带来没花巧噱头的传统粤菜，扎实的烹调功夫尽显四时食材真鲜味，烧味、小菜和老火汤深得食客欢迎，招牌菜有花胶杏汁炖白肺、沙姜陈皮生煎鸡等，不少人更爱于厢房以鲍鱼燕窝套餐宴客。

HONG KONG
香港

TEL.+852 2710 1093

B2F, Eaton Hotel, 380 Nathan Road, Jordan

佐敦弥敦道380号逸东酒店地库2楼

ASIA 亚洲

David Hartung/Yat Tung Heen

YEE TUNG HEEN
怡东轩

The first thing you'll notice is the Chinese ornaments and the second is how well Chinese screens and contemporary lighting go together. This elegant restaurant not only offers traditional Cantonese favourites but also serves specialities of a more creative persuasion. The enthusiastic chef and his team spend much time seeking out the best quality seasonal ingredients, whether that's from local markets or overseas.

踏入怡东酒店内的怡东轩中菜厅，马上便会给精致的中式摆设吸引。往内走，会发现四周的中式屏风与现代天花灯，配搭得十分别致。餐厅供应传统粤菜，厨师及营运团队充满热诚，专程由本地及世界各地搜罗各种高素质及时令食材，时有创新菜式或特别餐单推出。

HONG KONG
香港

TEL.+852 2837 6790

2F, The Excelsior Hotel, 281 Gloucester Road, Causeway Bay

铜锣湾告士打道281号怡东酒店2楼

Yee Tung Heen

YING JEE CLUB
营致会馆

Rather than gimmicky promotions, the owner prefers diverting more energy and resources to finding the freshest ingredients and refining the chef's cooking techniques. Diners are greeted by an elegant and contemporary dining hall adorned with marble tables, velvet seats and metallic trims. The menu is traditionally Cantonese with a touch of finesse. Their signature crispy salted chicken is silky and tender without being overly oily.

没有花巧和猛烈的宣传攻势，只以最新鲜的食材和熟练的烹调技巧为客人奉上传统而细致的广东菜，招牌菜脆香贵妃鸡皮脆酥香、肉质嫩滑且不油腻。以翡翠、云石、丝绒、金属框等物料作装潢陈设，感觉典雅时尚。

HONG KONG
香港

TEL.+852 2801 6882

Shop G05, 107-108, Nexxus Building, 41 Connaught Road Central, Central

中环干诺道中41号盈置大厦地下G05及1楼107-108号铺

www.yingjeeclub.hk

CHAN KAN KEE CHIU CHOW (SHEUNG WAN)
陈勤记卤鹅饭店（上环）

Ms Chan's grandfather set up this family business in 1948 in Sheung Wan; it moved to its current location in 1994 and was completely refurbished in 2010, when the kitchen was also expanded. Chiu Chow goose, cooked in a secret family recipe, remains the main event here, but there are other Chiu Chow specialities on offer such as pan fried baby oyster with egg, steamed goby fish with salted lemon, and double-boiled pig's lung and almond soup.

此店始创于1948年，由陈小姐的祖父于上环开创，1994年迁至现址，及后于2010年大规模翻新，除了厨房规模加以扩充，楼面亦一改容貌。以家传秘方炮制的潮州卤鹅仍然是招牌菜，另外还提供其他潮州特色美食，如潮州蚝仔粥、柠檬蒸乌鱼和杏汁炖白肺汤等。

HONG KONG
香港

TEL.+852 2858 0033
11 Queen's Road West, Sheung Wan
上环皇后大道西11号

CHIUCHOW DELICACIES
潮乐园

Walls covered in photos the chef took with celebrities speak volumes about the popularity of this no-frills shop. Velvety goose meat steeped in its signature spiced marinade, baby oyster porridge, oyster omelette, and pork blood curd with chives keep the regulars coming. Sourced from a local fish farm, the fatty grey mullet is juicy but without a muddy taste. It also serves rare traditional Chiu Chow gems, such as raw marinated red ark clams.

简朴的店子，墙上满是东主与厨师和名人的合照，其受欢迎程度不言而喻。卤水汁的香料成分有特定比例，因此，每天供应的卤水食物味道绝无差异。不含味精的卤汁令鹅肉更嫩滑。采用的乌头是元朗杨氏乌头，带黄油且没泥味。还供应时下较罕见的潮式生腌蜊蚶。蚝仔粥、蚝饼及韭菜猪红很受常客欢迎。

HONG KONG
香港

TEL.+852 3568 5643

GF, Ngan Fai Building, 84-94 Wharf Road, North Point
北角和富道84-94号银辉大厦地下

Chiuchow Delicacies

CHUEN CHEUNG KUI (MONG KOK)
泉章居（旺角）

This two-storey restaurant has been owned by the same family since the 1960s. It moved to this location in 2004 and has been jam-packed at night ever since. Diners line up to enjoy its traditional Hakkanese fare, including the unmissable salt-baked chicken and braised pork belly with dried mustard greens. The ground floor is smaller in size and rice plates that are less complicated to prepare are served there during lunch hours.

菜馆自六十年代起一直由同一家族经营，直至2004年才迁至现址。虽然餐厅楼高两层，但晚上经常座无虚席，门外排队等候的客人，为的都是这里的传统客家菜，不能错过的有盐焗鸡和梅菜扣肉。下层地铺面积较小，下午时分主要供应烹调工序较简单的盖浇饭。

HONG KONG
香港

TEL.+852 2396 0672
Lisa House, 33 Nelson Street, Mong Kok
旺角奶路臣街33号依利大厦

亞洲

ASIA

Michelin

FU SING (CAUSEWAY BAY)
富声（铜锣湾）

With its modern interior, attentive service and accessible location, it is little wonder that this large second Fu Sing restaurant has proved so successful. The dim sum selection is comprehensive and the prices are suitably appealing to allow for much over-ordering. Specialities include steamed crab in Chinese wine and soy sauce chicken in Fu Sing style, but we also recommend the garoupa with preserved vegetables and fish head soup in Shunde style.

富现代感的装潢，细心的服务，加上地点便利，难怪这间富声第二分店会如此成功！点心选择多且价钱合理，除了招牌菜富声花雕蒸蟹和鲍汁豉油鸡外，甜菜三葱炒斑球及顺德无骨鱼云羹同样值得一试。何不多点几道菜，与良朋好友共享美食？

HONG KONG
香港

TEL.+852 2504 4228

1F, 68 Yee Wo Street, Causeway Bay
铜锣湾怡和街68号1楼

Michelin

FU SING (WAN CHAI)
富声（湾仔）

Located in a commercial building in Wan Chai, the dining room of Fu Sing is modern and benefits from having a glass roof. The service team are attentive and the cooking, with its broad repertoire of Cantonese dishes, is undertaken with equal care. Dim sum is recommended, as is fish head soup in Shunde style, soy sauce chicken Fu Sing style, and steamed crab in Chinese wine.

富声位处时尚大楼之中，升降机可带你直达这富丽堂皇、占地宽广的酒家，采用玻璃天花的餐室设计风格富现代感。侍应服务非常周到，选择多元化的粤菜餐单，全属精心炮制之作。除了点心以外，推介菜式包括顺德无骨鱼云羹、富声鲍汁豉油鸡及花雕蒸蟹。

HONG KONG
香港

TEL.+852 2893 2228

3F, Sunshine Plaza, 353 Lockhart Road, Wan Chai
湾仔骆克道353号三湘大厦3楼

FUNG SHING (MONG KOK)
凤城（旺角）

This family business has been going since 1954; and their story has been published along with assorted recipes. Owner-chef Mr Tam looks to the region of Shunde for inspiration for his tasty Cantonese cooking – must try dishes are stir-fried milk with egg whites and roasted suckling pig. The two-storey restaurant is always busy, so it's well worth booking in advance.

HONG KONG
香港

TEL.+852 2381 5261
1-2F, 749 Nathan Road, Mong Kok
旺角弥敦道749号1-2楼

○日

这个由家族经营的生意始于1954年，位于旺角的这家总店共有两层，其历史与部分食谱已辑录成书出版。主厨兼东主谭国景从顺德菜中寻找烹调美味广东菜的灵感，大良炒鲜奶及驰名烧乳猪绝对值得一试。

GLORIOUS CUISINE
增辉艺厨

The live fish tank at the entrance is itself a spectacle – Hokkaido scallops, Thai marble goby, and even rare hanasaki crab if you're lucky, all to be cooked and served at your dining table. Apart from fish, the signature braised chicken stuffed with abalone and sea cucumber has also won the hearts of many. It is worth pre-ordering their roasted-to-order suckling pig and chicken marinated in first-press soy sauce.

北海道带子、泰国笋壳鱼……门外的鱼缸内是来自各地的海鲜,幸运的话,或能吃到日本花咲蟹。曾经营鸡只生意的东主,优势在能取得新鲜食材。自创的鲍鱼海参鸡,以鲍鱼和海参酿入鸡中,煮后再把汁液浸鸡,令其均匀入味,是他引以为傲之作。即烧BB乳猪及头抽鸡同样受欢迎,每晚限量供应,需预订。

HONG KONG
香港

TEL.+852 2778 8103

31-33 Shek Kip Mei Street, Sham Shui Po
深水埗石硖尾街31-33号

JU XING HOME
聚兴家

This hole-in-the-wall with only seven tables is always jam-packed – because of its food, not because of its décor or service. Regulars range from hotel chefs to local stars. Chef-owner Ng gets hands on in the kitchen and tries out new recipes with other cooks. The menu was mostly Cantonese at first, but now comes with a few Sichuan options. His succulent salt-baked chicken is a must-try. Reservations are highly recommended.

没有豪华装修，亦没有五星级服务，小店内只有七张餐桌，却经常满座，且是许多酒店大厨和明星的饭堂，因此想在此用餐，请务必订座。店东兼主厨吴师傅喜欢亲自下厨，亦爱与各大厨师交流并学习新菜式，由最初主攻粤菜到现在店内添加了少量川菜。用鲜鸡炮制的新鲜盐焗鸡是招牌菜。

HONG KONG
香港

TEL.+852 2392 9283

GF, 418 Portland Street, Prince Edward

太子砵兰街418号地下

KWAN KEE CLAY POT RICE
坤记煲仔小菜

Its typical greasy spoon-style interior and the traditional stir-fries it serves all point to an authentic Hong Kong culinary experience. Its famous clay pot rice is only served at night, and features a blend of three types of rice enrobed in oil brushed on the bottom of the clay pot. The rice itself is chewy and fragrant, with a crispy crust on the bottom perfectly scorched from the right amount of heat and time.

亲切而熟悉的饭店大门,是地道的香港风味,饭店供应的是传统港式小炒。只在晚上供应的驰名煲仔饭,饭底上了三种米混合而成,均匀地涂在瓦煲底的油渗透于饭内,米饭吃起来特别香滑软糯;控制得宜的时间与火候,令饭焦变得十分香脆。一口饭、一啖茶,幸福竟是如此简单!

TEL.+852 2803 7209

Shop 1, GF, Wo Yick Mansion, 263 Queen's Road West, Sai Ying Pun
西营盘皇后大道西263号和益大厦地下1号铺

LAN YUEN CHEE KOON
兰苑饎馆

The Chan's first place opened back in '84; they moved here in '98 to premises with a proper kitchen and now offer Cantonese claypots, healthy home-style steamed dishes, noodles and deliciously sweet puddings. Fine Chinese furniture is a feature of the small dining room, where Mrs Chan does the cooking and her husband the serving. The set menus at dinner prove particularly popular so be prepared to queue outside. It only serves dessert on Mondays.

陈氏夫妇创办的这家食馆，原店在1984年开业，并于1998年迁到有正规厨房的现址；雅致的中式家具是餐厅的特色。厨房由陈太掌舵，供应各种粤式煲仔菜、健康家常蒸煮菜式、面食、美味糕点和糖水。陈先生则负责招呼客人。晚饭时间的套餐特别受欢迎。周一只供应甜品。

TEL.+852 2381 1369

318 Sai Yeung Choi Street North, Prince Edward

太子西洋菜北街318号

Michelin

LIN HEUNG KUI
莲香居

This huge two-floor eatery opened in 2009 with the aim of building on the success of the famous Lin Heung Tea House in Wellington Street. It's modest inside but hugely popular and the dim sum trolley is a must, with customers keen to be the first to choose from its extensive offerings. The main menu offers classic Cantonese dishes with specialities such as Lin Heung special duck. Don't miss the limited offered pig lungs soup with almond juice. The pastry shop below is worth a look on the way out.

莲香居于2009年开业，楼高两层，延续威灵顿街莲香楼的辉煌成绩。朴素的内部装潢掩不住鼎沸的人气，以传统点心车盛载着各式各样经典点心，让人急不及待从中选择心头好，限量供应的杏汁白肺汤不能错过。菜单上罗列了传统广东菜及特色小菜，如莲香霸王鸭。离开时不妨逛逛楼下的中式饼店。

HONG KONG
香港

TEL.+852 2156 9328

2-3F, 40-50 Des Voeux Road West, Sheung Wan

上环德辅道西40-50号2-3楼

MEGAN'S KITCHEN
美味厨

HONG KONG
香港

TEL.+852 2866 8305

5F, Lucky Centre, 165-171 Wan Chai Road, Wan Chai
湾仔湾仔道165-171乐基中心5楼
www.meganskitchen.com

Those who like a little privacy while they eat will appreciate the booth seating with sliding screens – the restaurant underwent a renovation in 2016. The choice of Cantonese dishes is considerable and includes specialities like steamed minced beef with dried mandarin peel – and all dishes come with complimentary rice, soup and dessert. The restaurant is also known for its hotpots, which are made with good quality ingredients.

在广东菜和火锅中难以选择？美味厨让你不再苦恼。这儿除了有各式广东小菜如陈皮蒸手剁牛肉和美味煲仔饭外，火锅亦同样闻名，更有海鲜、和牛等高级火锅配料。点选小菜奉送汤、白饭和甜品，经济实惠。餐厅内的卡座设备齐全，拉下布幕即成私密度高的私人厢座。

Megan's Kitchen

PO KEE
波记

Po Kee is familiar to anyone who's lived in Western District as it's been a feature here for over 40 years and for many local residents a bowl of rice noodles (Lai Fan) with roasted duck leg remains a cherished childhood memory. To prepare his own roast meats, the owner built a factory behind the shop when he moved it to the current address. Regulars know to come before 2pm which is about the time the pork sells out each day.

西环的居民对波记一定不会陌生，此店在区内已有逾四十年历史，一碗美味的烧鸭腿濑粉是许多人的童年回忆。迁至现址后，店主在店铺后自设工场，炮制多款烧味。区内居民对店内各款美食了若指掌，烧肉往往在下午二时前售罄，欲试其烧鹅，最好在四时前到达。

HONG KONG
香港

425P Queen's Road West, Western District
西环皇后大道西425P号

SANG KEE
生记

Having stood here proudly for over 40 years, Sang Kee is a true symbol of Wan Chai and remains refreshingly impervious to modernisation. The owner insists on buying the seafood herself each day and the Cantonese dishes are prepared using traditional methods. You'll find yourself thinking about their classic dishes like fried snapper, fried minced pork with cuttlefish, and braised fish with bitter melon long after you've sampled them.

现在许多粤菜餐厅都以雷同的装潢和新派菜单作招徕，令生记这类传统酒家让人感到特别亲切！开业逾四十年，店主一直坚持每天亲自采购优质海鲜，以传统烹调方式制作一道道经典广东菜：用时令材料炮制的干煎海鳢，家常菜如土鱿煎肉饼和凉瓜炆鱼等，令人回味无穷。

HONG KONG
香港

TEL.+852 2575 2236

1-2F, Hip Sang Building, 107-115 Hennessy Road, Wan Chai

湾仔轩尼诗道107-115号协生大厦 1-2楼

www.sangkee.com.hk

ASIA 亚洲

Michelin

SHE WONG YEE
蛇王二

Their signature snake soup has long been renowned and on a typical winter's day over 1,000 bowls are served. Regulars are quick to occupy one of the few tables for this memorable experience and it is no surprise that the recipe has remained unchanged for years. These days, those regulars come also for the famed barbecued meats and homemade liver sausages; the roast goose and double-boiled soups are good too.

此店位于铜锣湾的中心地带，以传统方法烹调的蛇羹多年来口碑载道，秋冬高峰期更每日出售逾千碗。除此之外，其自制润肠也同样令食客趋之若鹜，而盅头滋补炖汤是不少本地市民的最爱。店内气氛热闹，需与其他人拼桌用膳。

HONG KONG
香港

TEL.+852 2831 0163
24 Percival Street, Causeway Bay
铜锣湾波斯富街24号

SHEK KEE KITCHEN
石记厨房

HONG KONG
香港

TEL.+852 2571 3348
GF, 15-17 Ngan Mok Street, Tin Hau
天后银幕街15-17号地下

It serves ordinary Cha Chaan Teng fare during the day, but turns into a dining hotspot specialising in home-style Cantonese dishes at night. The owner-chef sources the freshest ingredients from wet markets daily. Regulars also call him directly to pre-order certain dishes, including the signature fried chicken with toasted garlic that needs to be ordered one day ahead. Menu changes regularly to reflect the seasonal produce available.

餐厅在日间供应普通茶餐厅食物，而晚间却是人气鼎盛、主打家庭式广东小菜的菜馆。大厨兼东主每天会亲自往街市选购最新鲜的食材，部分熟客更会直接致电预订当晚的菜式，石记风沙鸡需要提前一天预订。菜单经常更新，确保所用的是最时令的食材。

SHEUNG HEI CLAYPOT RICE
尝囍煲仔小菜

Most claypot rice in town is cooked to order – but this shop takes it one step further and does it on a charcoal stove. The rice has a characteristic smoky scent with a crispy crust at the bottom. Order the one with eel and pork ribs for the rich aroma of the fish and the luscious pork grease that coats every grain. The owner also runs a dim sum shop next door where you can order some Cantonese bite-size munchies to go with your claypot rice.

即点即煮并非这儿的特别之处，倒是其碳烤煲仔饭的方法使人印象深刻。以碳火烹煮米饭时香气已扑鼻而来，煮熟后的饭焦更加香味诱人。推介白鳝排骨饭，能吃到鳝的香味之余，排骨内的油分渗进饭内令米饭变得更香软。隔邻的点心店是姊妹店，食客可以选些点心佐餐。

HONG KONG
香港

TEL.+852 2819 6190
GF, 25 North Street, Western District
西环北街25号地下

Sheung Hei Claypot Rice

SING KEE (CENTRAL)
星记（中环）

The second branch of Sing Kee is a bright, tidy spot serving classic Cantonese food – something that's proving increasingly hard to find in Central. You'll find only traditional recipes using chicken, pork and seafood here, free of gimmicks or fancy presentation. Many specialities need pre-ordering, like chicken with ginger in clam sauce, or almond juice with fish maw and pig's lung. Come at lunch to take advantage of some reasonable prices.

想在中环区找到提供朴实高质的传统粤菜且环境干净整洁的餐馆，星记便是你的选择。选用新鲜肉类如猪、鸡及生猛海鲜等食材加上扎实的烹调技术，自然不乏支持者。午市提供一系列价钱实惠的小菜，甚得中环人士欢心。建议预订炖汤如杏汁花胶炖猪肺。

HONG KONG
香港

TEL.+852 2970 0988

2F, 1 Lyndhurst Tower, 1 Lyndhurst Terrace, Central
中环摆花街1号一号广场2楼

Michelin

SIU SHUN VILLAGE CUISINE (KOWLOON BAY)

肇顺名汇河鲜专门店（九龙湾）

Not only do the river fish swim in the fish tanks at the entrance, but also in the waterways under the tempered glass floor – diners might even be under the illusion that they are dining in a glass-bottom boat on a river. It specialises in Shunde regional cooking and river fish dishes, including fried giant prawns with ginger and spring onion, stir-fried beef tenderloin strips with mushrooms in XO sauce, and braised fish lips casserole.

门外大大小小的鱼缸放满各式各样的河鲜，走到店内亦不难发现脚下有水道和强化玻璃，鱼儿在客人的脚下游来游去，特别的设计仿佛要提醒客人这里的河鲜不能错过。很多本地食客特意到此品尝顺德菜及河鲜菜式，招牌菜包括姜葱大虾球、XO酱双菇牛柳条和瓦罉煎焗鱼咀等。

HONG KONG
香港

TEL.+852 2798 9738

Shop 6, 7F, MegaBox, 38 Wang Chiu Road, Kowloon Bay

九龙湾宏照道38号MegaBox7楼6号铺

SUN YUEN HING KEE
新园兴记

Located next to Sheung Wan market, this traditionally styled, simple but well maintained barbecue shop has been run by the same family since the mid-1970s. Over the years they've built up an appreciative following so the small place fills quickly. The appetising looking suckling pigs are not the only draw: roast pork, duck and pigeon all have their followers, as do the soft-boiled chicken, the homemade sausages and the preserved meats.

位于上环街市旁边，这间格调传统简单的烧味店自七十年代中一直由同一家族经营。多年来，累积了不少忠实顾客，小小的地方往往座无虚席。这里受欢迎的不仅是挂在厨房旁边，卖相令人垂涎欲滴的乳猪，烧肉、烤鸭和乳鸽都各有忠实捧场客。白切鸡、腊肠及腊肉亦十分吸引。

ASIA 亚洲

HONG KONG
香港

TEL.+852 2541 2207

327-329 Queen's Road Central, Sheung Wan

上环皇后大道中327-329号

Michelin

TAI WING WAH
大荣华

A refit in 2016 resulted in this Cantonese restaurant, located in the north of New Territories, looking a little brighter and feeling a little fresher. It serves dim sum and 'Walled Village' cuisine, alongside assorted classic Cantonese dishes. Try the roast duck with bean paste and coriander; claypot rice with lard and premium soy sauce; and, above all, the steamed sponge cake.

很多人长途跋涉来到元朗,只有一个原因:光顾大荣华。此酒家除了供应点心外,还提供近百款围村小菜及经典粤式名菜如香茜烧米鸭及钵仔猪油头抽捞饭等,还有奶黄马拉糕。翻新过的餐厅用上五彩缤纷的地毯和明亮的灯光,配上传统装饰,感觉焕然一新。

HONG KONG
香港

TEL.+852 2476 9888
2F, 2-6 On Ning Road, Yuen Long
元朗安宁路2-6号2楼

&. ⟷

ASIA 亚洲

TAI WOO (CAUSEWAY BAY)
太湖海鲜城（铜锣湾）

One of the district's most famous names, Tai Woo moved to these more comfortable surroundings in 2011 and, while the restaurant may be smaller than before, business is better than ever, with over 1,000 customers served every day. What hasn't changed is the quality of the service or the cooking – along with a menu of Cantonese seafood dishes, such as crunchy shrimp ball and mini lobster casserole, are favourites like sesame chicken baked in salt.

HONG KONG
香港

TEL.+852 2893 0822

9F, Causeway Bay Plaza 2, 463-483 Lockhart Road, Causeway Bay

铜锣湾骆克道463-483号铜锣湾广场第二期9楼

www.taiwoorestaurant.com

☐ ◑⫽

于八十年代开业的太湖是区内驰名酒家，尤擅海鲜菜式，2011年才搬迁到更新更舒适的现址。多年来食物素质维持不变，生意昌旺每天服务逾千名食客，即便如此，服务依然周到。这里提供多款广东菜式，招牌菜有芝麻盐焗鸡、奇脆明珠伴金龙及姜米鲜鱼炒饭等。

TAK KEE
德记

It started out as a street-side hawker stall in the 1980s and still retains the casual, vibrant vibe. The second-generation hands-on owner shops for groceries every day and sometimes helps the experienced chefs with kitchen chores. Pork tripe and peppercorn soup is a culinary highlight, using berries from Malaysia and Indonesia. Regulars also come for its spiced marinated goose liver, crispy chitterlings stuffed with glutinous rice and oyster omelette.

于八十年代开业，早期为大牌档，现由第二代经营。店东凡事亲力亲为，每天亲自到菜市场采购新鲜食材，间或会在厨房帮忙潮州老师傅打点厨务。这儿的胡椒猪肚汤独特之处是采用马来西亚和印尼两种胡椒，卤水大鹅肝、脆皮糯米酿大肠及驰名蚝仔饼深得食客喜爱。传统荷包鳝，需最少八位或以上才接受预订。

HONG KONG
香港

TEL.+852 2819 5568

GF, 3 G Belcher's Street, Western District
西环卑路乍街3号G地铺

Tak Kee

TRUSTY GOURMET
信得过

The owner also runs a company supplying pork so he has an edge on sourcing the freshest pork at competitive prices. He believes the quality of the food speaks louder than fame and doesn't allow MSG in the kitchen. The signature stir-fried pork offal with salted mustard greens boasts offal from 12- to 14-month-old pigs for tenderness. Diners also rave about the thickly sliced pork liver and the pork lung soup with almond milk.

猪肉供应商的家族背景,令店东在货源上占有优势,确保猪肉新鲜和有素质。注重食品素质多于名气的店东不仅实行无味精烹调方式,还选用12至14个月大的中猪作猪杂材料,肉质较幼嫩。厚切猪肝是此店的特色食品,较受食客喜爱的有杏汁白肺汤、咸菜炒猪杂、彩椒炒肥牛肠和奇妙肚丝蛋钵。

HONG KONG
香港

TEL.+852 2838 7373

Shop A, Fasteem Mansion, 307-311 Jaffe Road, Wan Chai

湾仔谢斐道307-311号快添大厦A铺

YIXIN
益新

North Point was the original location for this family-run restaurant when it opened in the 1950s. It's moved a few times since then but is now firmly ensconced here in Wan Chai. Run by the 3rd generation of the family, a sense of continuity also comes from the head chef who has been with the company over 50 years! The Cantonese food is traditional, with quite a few Shunde dishes; specialities include roasted duck Pipa-style, and smoked pomfret.

早于五十年代于港岛区开业，辗转搬至湾仔现址，现由第三代经营。益新一向以传统粤菜驰名，餐单上不乏耗功夫制作的怀旧菜式，吸引不少客人在此举行宴会。琵琶鸭、金钱鸡及烟焗鲳鱼等都是常客所爱。除了地面的主厅和客房外，地库还有一个装潢时尚的餐室。

HONG KONG
香港

TEL.+852 2834 9963
50 Hennessy Road, Wan Chai
湾仔轩尼诗道50号

ASIA 亚洲

YUE KEE
裕记

Since its humble beginnings as a tiny countryside joint 60 years ago, this second-generation family business has grown substantially while still retaining its unique flair. Geese are sourced from eight different farms in China to ensure quality and a steady supply. The owner insists on chargrilling the geese, according to his family recipe, for distinctive smokiness, crispy skin and juicy meat. Apart from geese, seafood and stir-fries are also served.

HONG KONG
香港

TEL.+852 2491 0105
9 Sham Hong Road, Sham Tseng
深井深康路9号
www.yuekee.com.hk

开业六十年，从乡村小店到现在的规模，仍保留着传统食店风味。现由第二代打理。采用的鹅是从内地八个农场合作伙伴中挑选，确保鹅肉的货源和素质，店主多年来坚持按家传秘方以炭火烤制烧鹅，味道独特且酥香肉嫩。现更增设海鲜及特色小菜，让食客有更多选择。

YUET LAI SHUN
粤来顺

Ceiling fans, window grilles, booth seats and faux-marble tables are reminiscent of the good old cha chaan teng in Hong Kong circa 1960s. The décor also chimes with the food it serves – retro Cantonese classics that are well-made and reasonably priced. Chicken poached in honey soy stands out, with juicy velvety meat and well-balanced sauce. Deep-fried shrimp balls with cheese filling and pork lung almond milk soup are among diners' favourites.

吊扇加铁窗花、带点茶餐厅味道的云石方桌卡座，装潢一如六、七十年代的酒楼，很有老香港风情。与其装潢一样，这儿主打的就是怀旧广东菜。蜂蜜豉油鸡肉质嫩滑，与以虾胶芝士作馅料的千丝芝心球和生磨杏汁白肺汤同属招牌菜。

HONG KONG
香港

TEL.+852 2788 3078
Shop 10-12, GF Po Hang Building, 2-8 Dundas Street, Mong Kok
旺角登打士街2-8号宝亨大厦地下 10-12号铺

YUNG KEE
容记小菜王

Moved to this new location in 2017, this bustling hawker-style joint attracts crowds who jam its entrance every night. Regulars come for their traditional Cantonese fare including home-style braised pork belly and baked fish tripe omelette in an earthenware bowl, both of which are limited in offer. Make sure you book ahead and show up on time. Walk-in guests should expect to wait for at least an hour.

店子于2017年由深水埗迁至现址，每晚皆吸引许多食客在门外轮候，因为他们全是熟客。建议各位预早订座并切记准时到达，否则或要等候一个小时或以上才能入座。菜馆主打传统粤菜，招牌菜包括家乡秘制扣肉和家乡焗鱼肠，熟客都知道这两道菜式皆限量供应。

HONG KONG
香港

TEL.+852 2363 9380

GF & 1F, 123 Prince Edward Road West, Prince Edward
太子太子道西123号地下及1楼

 ♿ ⚙🍴

ABOVE & BEYOND
天外天

When your restaurant has been designed by Sir Terence Conran, it's a racing certainty it will be a stylish place – and that is indeed the case here on the 28th floor of the Hotel Icon. What is somewhat unexpected is finding Cantonese food being served in such surroundings. Signature dishes include wok-fried sea cucumber with spring onion; crispy crab claw with shrimp mousse; and prawns with tangerine peel and fermented black beans.

由泰伦斯·康爵(Sir Terence Conran)设计的唯港荟中菜厅,时尚典雅的酒吧大厅,是其一贯的设计风格,加上醉人的维港景致,叫人赞叹不已,临窗的座位无疑是最佳选择。在装潢如此西化的餐厅,提供的是添有现代元素的粤菜,招牌菜包括陈皮豆豉炒虾球、葱烧海参等。午市供应点心套餐。

HONG KONG
香港

TEL.+852 3400 1318

28F, Hotel Icon, 17 Science Museum Road, East Tsim Sha Tsui

尖东科学馆道17号唯港荟28楼

www.hotel-icon.com/dining/above-beyond

ASIA 亚洲

Above & Beyond

CELESTIAL COURT
天宝阁

The room may be windowless but that at least puts the emphasis on the decoration – which features plenty of wood veneer – and, of course, onto the food. The chef has over 40 years of Cantonese culinary experience and also spent time in Japan – and his cooking is informed by his travels. Specialities include roasted whole suckling pig with pearl barley and black truffles; and deep-fried prawns with spicy termite mushrooms and crispy rice toast.

天宝阁位于喜来登酒店内，虽然餐室欠窗户，但典雅堂皇的装潢和具水准的菜肴足以弥补。主厨于不同粤菜餐厅和日本打拼超过四十年，游历于不同城市也丰富了他的创作，黑松露薏米烧酿乳猪和饭焦鸡瑽菌凤尾虾是其得意之作。

HONG KONG
香港

TEL.+852 2732 6991

2F, Sheraton Hotel, 20 Nathan Road, Tsim Sha Tsui

尖沙咀弥敦道20号喜来登酒店2楼

www.sheratonhongkonghotel.com

ASIA 亚洲

Celestial Court

CHE'S
车氏粤菜轩

This unremarkable-looking little restaurant is popular with the local businessmen who come here in their droves for speedy service of the house speciality – crispy pork buns. But there are other reasons to visit: the dim sum at lunch; the extensive menu of classic dishes like crispy chicken or crab and dry scallop soup with bitter melon; simpler offerings such as congee or braised claypot dishes; and the blueberry pudding with which to end.

HONG KONG
香港

TEL.+852 2528 1123

4F, The Broadway, 54-62 Lockhart Road, Wan Chai

湾仔骆克道54-62号博汇大厦4楼

这家小餐馆看似不起眼，但在本地商界人士间却享负盛名，选择丰富的经典粤菜如脆皮炸子鸡，简单却美味的粥品和煲仔菜，还有午市点心，都使一众食客趋之若鹜。服务快速且有效率，午餐时分往往座无虚席。

CHINA TANG (CENTRAL)
唐人馆（中环）

HONG KONG
香港

TEL.+852 2522 2148

**Shop 411-413, 4F, Landmark Atrium,
15 Queen's Road Central, Central**

中环皇后大道中15号置地广场4楼
411-413号铺

www.chinatang.hk

Decorated with a mix of traditional Chinese art and contemporary Western design, this handsome restaurant was conceived and designed by Sir David Tang as a sister to the London branch. Tables are set closely together and there are several private rooms. Dishes from Beijing, Sichuan and Canton feature and dim sum is popular. The most recently appointed chef hasn't tinkered too much with the menu, although he has introduced a more modern element.

由邓永锵爵士构思及设计，是其继伦敦唐人馆后又一杰作。人手刺绣的墙纸、独特的镜饰、古董灯饰及线装中式排版菜谱，中式传统艺术与西方美学结合得天衣无缝，流露出典雅贵气。菜单涵盖粤、京、川等地美食及精制南北点心；老北京传统挂炉烤鸭、唐人馆叉烧和琉璃虾球等，滋味无穷。

China Tang

CHINA TANG (HARBOUR CITY)
唐人馆（海港城）

In 2016 Hong Kong got its second China Tang, this time in Harbour City. A bar and lounge with pretty embroidery and chinoiserie fabrics leads into the colourful, comfortable dining room. Some appetizers are prepared by a chef from Hangzhou; traditional Beijing roast duck comes courtesy of a Beijinese chef. Recommendations include marinated shrimps with 'Hua Diao' wine, crystal prawns with lobster bisque, and wok-fried dried beef with onions.

HONG KONG
香港

唐人馆在香港的第二家分店，同样由邓永锵爵士设计。他巧妙地将欧陆式装潢和中式元素融合，色彩缤纷的布料搭配优雅的花卉图案，雅致舒适。餐单以粤菜为主，也有南北点心、佐酒小食和大筐地炉端烧菜式；厨师团队包括杭州的凉菜师傅和北京的烤鸭师傅。陈年花雕话梅虾和琥珀水晶大虾球值得一试。

TEL.+852 2157 3148

Shop 4101, 4F, Gateway Arcade, Harbour City, 17 Canton Road, Tsim Sha Tsui
尖沙咀广东道17号海港城港威商场4楼4101号铺
www.chinatang.hk

ASIA 亚洲

CHINESE LEGEND
广东名门

Located right opposite the seafood market, this popular glass-walled restaurant not only cooks the critters you get from the market, but also serves their own famous Cantonese roast meat, such as lychee wood-roasted goose, available in a limited daily quantity daily. Despite its plain interior, antique pieces add some interest and there is even a stone grinder hidden underneath each round table.

门上刻有"广东名门"的牌匾是店主从广东运来，是菜馆名字的由来。位处海鲜市场，客人会先购买海鲜，再拿到菜馆前台的篮子量重并作记号。每晚都人头涌涌轮候入座，不仅是为了烹调出色的海鲜，还为了以荔枝柴熏烤的各款烧味，如限量供应的荔枝柴烧鹅。店内有许多古董家具，连圆形桌子底部都藏了一个石磨，煞是有趣。

HONG KONG
香港

TEL.+852 2955 1313

Shop 1, GF, Sam Shing Market, Sam Shing Estate
屯门三圣村三圣市场1号地下
www.kingmen.com.hk

ASIA 亚洲

Michelin

🍴⃝

COME-INTO CHIU CHOW
金燕岛

The restaurant may have moved in 2014 but that hasn't stopped all the regulars coming along for their regular fix of Chao Zhou dishes. The team spirit of the staff, many of whom have been working together for over three decades, is clear to see and the restaurant itself has quite a grand feel and comes complete with assorted calligraphy and paintings. The standout Chao Zhou dishes include bird's nest and soyed meat such as goose web and wings.

餐厅在2014年迁至现址，共占两层，二楼有多间设备齐全的厢房，一楼的主餐室饰以书画作品，装潢甚具中式大宅气派。由早年在星光行开业起，此店一直以高级潮州菜驰名，共事已久的员工默契十足，熟客也追随至今。驰名潮州美食有燕窝菜式和卤味如卤水鹅掌翼。

HONG KONG
香港

TEL.+852 2322 0020

1F & 2F, Guang Dong Hotel, 18 Prat Avenue, Tsim Sha Tsui
尖沙咀宝勒巷18号粤海酒店1-2楼
www.come-into.com.hk

♿ 🍽 🆗🍴

🍴

CUISINE CUISINE AT THE MIRA
国金轩 (THE MIRA)

HONG KONG
香港

TEL.+852 2315 5222

3F, The Mira Hotel, 118 Nathan Road, Tsim Sha Tsui

尖沙咀弥敦道118号The Mira 3楼

www.themirahotel.com

🐾 ♿ 🚪 🥢 🅿 🍽

Striking crystal orbs hanging down from above make quite a statement at this stylish dining room on the 3rd floor of the equally fashionable Mira hotel. It'll come as little surprise to learn that the Cantonese cooking also comes with modern touches. Dim sum is good but to see the kitchen at its best try specialities like soft shell crab, pumpkin soup with winter melon, and Peking duck – given a twist with three flavoured pancakes.

这家充满现代感的型格餐厅位于同样时尚的The Mira酒店三楼,圆球状的水晶吊灯引人注目,在此享受融入精巧现代元素的广东美食,可谓相得益彰。午市供应精美点心,然而自选菜式更能体验厨房的功力,东方夜明珠和芝麻桔子软壳蟹都值得一试,北京片皮鸭两食配以三款特色薄饼,口味创新。

Cuisine Cuisine at the Mira

DRAGON KING (KWUN TONG)
龙皇（观塘）

Creative Cantonese dishes with a seafood slant are the draw at this contemporary dining room owned by famous local chef Wong Wing Chee. Standout dishes include Australian Tiger Jade abalone double-boiled with herbs, and Mantis prawns steamed in a bamboo basket. From time to time the chefs enter group culinary competitions to aid their cooking skills and creative thinking – the results can be seen in some of the more innovative dishes on the menu.

这家富现代感的中菜馆，提供以海鲜为主的创新广东菜式，东主为香港著名厨师黄永帜。在芸芸美食中，最出众的有石决明炖老虎鲍和清蒸斑马富贵虾。所属集团会定期举行厨艺比赛，让各分店主厨施展实力与创意，同时亦会将搭配新颖的得奖菜式上市供食客品尝。

HONG KONG
香港

TEL.+852 2955 0668
2F, Yen Sheng Centre, 64 Hoi Yuen Road, Kwun Tong
观塘开源道64号源成中心2楼
www.dragonkinggroup.com

ASIA
亚洲

Dragon King

DRAGON NOODLES ACADEMY
龙面馆

The wooden dummies, weapon racks, lion dance heads and hand-carved golden dragon pay homage to Hong Kong pop culture and kung fu studios circa 1970s. Apart from noodles, such as the Lanzhou variety, one of the most-ordered items, it also showcases an array of Chinese cooking with the creative use of Western ingredients and cooking techniques. Diners get to enjoy the performance of hand-pulling noodles in the open kitchen while sipping cocktails.

以七十年代武馆概念加中国特色陈设的装潢：木人桩、兵器架、舞狮头、手工雕刻金龙及旧式凉茶壶等，带有浓浓的中国特色。菜式却采用西化食材和加入了创新烹调风格，手打兰州拉面是常获食客点选的食品。开放式厨房，让拉面师傅的制面和拉面绝技毫无保留地展现在食客眼前。店内还有供应鸡尾酒。

HONG KONG
香港

TEL.+852 2561 6688

Shop G04, GF, Man Yee Arcade, Man Yee Building, 68 Des Voeux Road Central, Central
中环德辅道中68号万宜大厦万宜廊地下G04号铺

www.dragon-noodles.com

ASIA 亚洲

Dragon Noodles Academy

FARM HOUSE
农圃

Set in a sleek business building, this
contemporary dining room has private rooms
leading off it as well as an eye-catching
aquarium running the entire length of one
wall. A highlight of the Cantonese menu is the
deep-fried chicken wing stuffed with glutinous
rice, while other specialities include the baked
sea whelk with goose liver, and steamed rice
with abalone and dried chicken. Many of the
ingredients are also available to buy.

饭店装潢时尚,进门便可看到数间贵宾房和一个
延伸整堵墙的巨型水族箱,非常引人注目。农圃的
粤菜选用特级新鲜材料炮制而成,著名菜式有古
法糯米鸡翼、鹅肝焗酿响螺和瑶柱鲍鱼鸡粒饭。
饭店亦出售一些难于家中烹调的食物如鲍鱼及海
参。

HONG KONG
香港

TEL.+852 2881 1331

1F, China Taiping Tower, 8 Sunning
Road, Causeway Bay
铜锣湾新宁道8号中国太平大厦1楼
www.farmhouse.com.hk

FOOK LAM MOON (WAN CHAI)
福临门（湾仔）

Run with considerable passion by the third generation of the same family, Fook Lam Moon is one of the best known restaurants around and attracts many regulars. Decoration of the two large dining rooms is based around a colour scheme of gold, silver and bronze which seems appropriate as there are so many luxury items on the menu. The respect for the ingredients is palpable and signature dishes include baked stuffed crab shell and roast suckling pig.

福临门意指好运来到你家门，现由创业家族的第三代经营，是城中享负盛名的酒家之一，深受一众食家爱戴。店内两个大堂以金、银、铜色系装潢，映衬着菜单上的珍馐百味。食材明显经过精心处理，招牌菜包括酿焗鲜蟹盖与大红片皮乳猪。

HONG KONG
香港

TEL.+852 2866 0663
35-45 Johnston Road, Wan Chai
湾仔庄士敦道35-45号
www.fooklammoon-grp.com

marcus tse/Fook Lam Moon

GOLDEN LEAF
金叶庭

Teak, rosewood, antique vases, lanterns and silks combine to make this very smart dining room as elegant as it is intimate. With no views to draw away your gaze, the Cantonese cuisine is allowed to take centre stage. Expect barbecued specialities like suckling pig, and pork with queen's honey, alongside seafood dishes like prawns in Chinese wine, and baked lobster with ginger. To dream of golden leaves is indeed a good omen.

金叶庭位于港丽酒店之内，饰以屏风、柚木树、古董花瓶、灯笼和丝绸画作的餐室，感觉高贵典雅。在充满东方情调的环境下，客人可以享受一系列传统广东菜肴，太白醉翁鸽、化皮乳猪件、蜜糖汁叉烧都叫人垂涎不已。

HONG KONG
香港

TEL.+852 2822 8570

5F, Conrad Hotel, Pacific Place, 88 Queensway, Admiralty

金钟道88号太古广场港丽酒店5楼

www.conraddining.com

ASIA 亚洲

Golden Leaf

HONG KONG
香港

TEL.+852 2450 6331

5 Sam Shing Street, Castle Peak Bay, Tuen Mun

屯门青山湾三圣街5号

♿ 🥢 **P** 🍴

HOI TIN GARDEN
海天花园

One of the biggest and best known restaurants on the seafood street in Sam Shing, this three-storey establishment, complete with its own parking lot, has been in business for over 30 years. Seafood lovers travel from around town to shop for their favourite catch at the wet market nearby and ask their chefs to cook it up. Dim sum is served in the morning. A private room on the third floor caters to bigger parties.

位于三圣村海鲜街入口,称得上是该处规模最大的酒家,楼高三层且设有停车场,街坊对海天这个名字一定不会感到陌生,概因她已在区内开业逾三十年。与海鲜街毗邻的便利,食客都会在市场购买海鲜后带到酒家内由厨师烹调处理。上午有早茶点心供应。一大班朋友聚餐,可选择在三楼的厢房。

Michelin

🍴

LEI GARDEN (IFC)
利苑酒家（国际金融中心）

Forward planning is advisable here – not only when booking but also when selecting certain roast meat dishes and some of their famous double-boiled soups which require advance notice. The extensive menu features specialist seafood dishes and the lunchtime favourites include shrimp and flaky pastries filled with shredded turnip. All this is served up by an efficient team, in clean, contemporary surroundings.

到这间利苑分店用餐，无论座位，还是食物如烧味或受欢迎的炖汤，均须提早预约。这里菜式种类繁多，其中以海鲜炮制的佳肴最具特色，而午市时段的美食首推巧制点心如银萝千层酥。格局设计富时代气息，洁净雅致，服务效率亦十分高。

HONG KONG
香港

TEL.+852 2295 0238

Shop 3008-3011, Podium Level 3, IFC Mall, 1 Harbour View Street, Central

中环港景街1号国际金融中心商场
第2期3楼3008-3011号铺

www.leigarden.com.hk

&. ⇔ ☺🍴

HONG KONG
香港

TEL.+852 2331 3306

Shop Unit F2, Telford Plaza 1, 33 Wai Yip Street, Kowloon Bay

九龙湾伟业街33号德福广场一期 F2号铺

www.leigarden.com.hk

LEI GARDEN (KOWLOON BAY)
利苑酒家（九龙湾）

Service is one of the strengths of this Lei Garden, located in a shopping mall near the MTR station. Signature dishes include the 10 different varieties of double-boiled tonic soups (to be ordered in advance), sautéed scallops with macadamia nuts and yellow fungus, and braised boneless spare-ribs with sweet and sour sauce. Those who like to eat lunch early or at pace are rewarded with a discount if they vacate their tables before 12:45pm.

这家利苑分店位于地铁站附近的商场内，服务周到是其强项。招牌菜包括多款须提前预订的炖汤、米网黄耳夏果炒带子、宫庭酱烤骨。中午12:45前离席有折扣优惠，对于喜欢提早吃午饭或能于短时间内吃毕午饭的顾客而言，这待遇确实吸引。

LEI GARDEN (SHA TIN)
利苑酒家（沙田）

It may have been in town for over 20 years, however, refurbishment has kept this Lei Garden feeling fresh. It is located in New Town Plaza Sha Tin, which means that it can get especially busy at weekends when everyone needs refuelling after a day spent shopping. The menu largely follows the theme of others in the group; always ask for the daily special. Pre-ordering the seasonal double-boiled tonic soup is particularly recommended.

位于沙田新城市广场的利苑分店已开业超过二十年，凭着精心烹调的正宗粤菜及舒适的室内环境，在区内蛮受食客欢迎，常常座无虚席。细心的服务员会在你致电订座时提醒你预订老火汤或时令特色小菜。

HONG KONG
香港

TEL.+852 2698 9111

Shop 628, 6F, Phase I New Town Plaza, Sha Tin
沙田新城市广场第1期6楼628号铺
www.leigarden.com.hk

ASIA 亚洲

Graham Uden/Lei Garden

LEI GARDEN (WAN CHAI)
利苑酒家（湾仔）

An inventory of restaurants in Wan Chai wouldn't be complete without a Lei Garden. This branch is bigger than most and boasts a busy, bustling atmosphere, particularly at lunchtime. It follows the group's tried-and-tested formula by offering an extensive menu of dishes with luxurious dishes alongside less elaborate but classic Cantonese specialities. Seafood enthusiasts should consider pre-ordering the Alaskan king crab or Brittany blue lobster.

论湾仔区的出色食肆，当然少不了利苑的份儿。菜单包含珍馐百味与经典粤式小菜，种类繁多，加上巧手精制的点心和便利的地点，难怪总是座无虚席。食客可于订位时跟店方预订特别海鲜如亚拉斯加蟹和法国蓝龙虾等。

HONG KONG
香港

TEL.+852 2892 0333

1F, CNT Tower, 338 Hennessy Road, Wan Chai
湾仔轩尼诗道338号北海中心1楼
www.leigarden.com.hk

ASIA 亚洲

Lei Garden

GAC MOTOR | THE ROAD TO GREATNESS

Dare to Dream
If dreams always stayed as dreams,
there would be no reason to dream.

From Ordinary to Extraordinary.
Make the Leap

敢　梦　想
梦想如果只是梦想
就没有存在的意义

平凡到伟大

LUK YU TEA HOUSE
陆羽茶室

Large numbers of both regulars and tourists come to Luk Yu Tea House for the traditionally prepared and flavoursome dim sum, and its three floors fill up quickly. The animated atmosphere and subtle colonial decoration are appealing but no one really stays too long; the serving team in white jackets have seen it all before and go about their work with alacrity. Popular dishes are fried prawns on toast and fried noodles with sliced beef.

陆羽茶室以传统方法制作的美味点心,不光招徕本地常客,更令不少外地游客慕名而至,所以楼高三层的茶室经常满座。生气盎然的环境和带点殖民地色彩的装潢别具特色,穿着白色外套的侍应敏捷而专注地工作。除点心外,其他菜式如窝贴虾及干炒牛河也值得一试。

HONG KONG
香港

TEL.+852 2523 5464
24-26 Stanley Street, Central
中环士丹利街24-26号

ONE HARBOUR ROAD
港湾壹号

One Harbour Road may be set in a hotel, but its graceful ambience will make you think you're on the terrace of an elegant 1930s Taipan mansion. Split-level dining adds to the airy feel, there are views of the harbour, and the sound of the fountain softens the bold statement of the huge pillars. Cantonese menus offer a wide variety of well-prepared meat and fish dishes. Private parties should consider booking the Chef's Table.

HONG KONG
香港

TEL.+852 2584 7722

8F, Grand Hyatt Hotel, 1 Harbour Road, Wan Chai
湾仔港湾道1号君悦酒店8楼
www.hongkong.grand.hyatt.com

这里的气氛，令你仿如置身三十年代的优雅大班府第。分层用餐，空间感较大，且能饱览维港景色。大型莲花池及潺潺的流水声，使感觉硬朗的大柱子变得柔和。这里的粤菜包括精心准备、种类繁多的肉类和鱼类菜式。如想一睹烹调过程，可考虑预订"厨师餐桌"。

One Harbour Road

PAK LOH CHIU CHOW (HYSAN AVENUE)

百乐潮州（希慎道）

There are now four branches of this Chao Zhou restaurant in Hong Kong, but this is the original – which was founded in 1967. For lunch try the baby oyster congee or the fried noodle with sugar and vinegar; in the evening you can go for something a little heavier like soyed goose liver. It's also worth pre-ordering a speciality, like deep-fried king prawn with bread noodles, and finishing with the classic Chao Zhou dessert of fried taro with sugar.

自1967年于铜锣湾开业，发展至今已有多间分店，而希慎道这间老店的受欢迎程度始终如一。食客最爱的菜式包括各式卤水食物如鹅肝及鹅，还有高质冻蟹，或者预订特别菜式如子母龙须虾、姜米乳鸽及荷包猪肚鸡汤等等。

HONG KONG
香港

TEL.+852 2576 8886

GF, 23-25 Hysan Avenue, Causeway Bay
铜锣湾希慎道23-25号

ASIA 亚洲

147

PAK LOH CHIU CHOW
(TIME SQUARE)
百乐潮州（时代广场）

A vaulted ceiling, clever lighting, woods and leather all combine to create a striking contemporary restaurant on the 10th floor of Times Square. The Chao Zhou cuisine is prepared in a traditional way using authentic ingredients, although the presentation – like the room – is modern. For lunch try dim sum or something light, such as sliced pomfret or baby oyster congee; for dinner the stewed, dried Oma abalone is a must.

HONG KONG
香港

TEL.+852 2577 1163

10F, Time Square, 1 Matheson Street, Causeway Bay

铜锣湾勿地臣街1号时代广场10楼

由香港年轻设计师操刀的室内设计，灯光、线条和空间构成出色的视觉效果，令人留下深刻印象。百乐这家分店提供一众传统潮州美食，配以精美外形，且份量较小巧容你可尝味更多。煎鲳鱼和卤水鹅当然不能少，想试点特别的食物可预先通知店家，让大厨为你炮制潮州烧响螺。

ASIA 亚洲

SEVENTH SON
家全七福

There was a change of venue for this Cantonese restaurant in 2016 – it is now housed on the 3rd floor of the Wharney Guang Dong Hotel. Its new surroundings are smart and contemporary, with gold and yellow colours adding warmth to the comfortable room. The standard of the traditional Cantonese cuisine remains as was, with the kitchen making good use of quality ingredients. The specialities are barbecued suckling pig and crispy chicken.

餐厅名称包含了东主父亲的名字及其在兄弟中的排序，也有传承父亲厨艺之意。从杜老志道迁至华美粤海酒店，新店以深色木地板配金黄色的日式装潢，感觉时尚。自十四岁随父习厨、擅长高级功夫粤菜的东主，以时令食材、最少的调味料和精细的烹调，带出食物真味。大红片皮乳猪和炸子鸡是招牌菜。

HONG KONG
香港

TEL.+852 2892 2888

3F, The Wharney Guang Dong Hotel HK, 57-73 Lockhart Road, Wan Chai
湾仔骆克道57-73号香港华美粤海酒店3楼

www.seventhson.hk

ASIA
亚洲

HONG KONG
香港

TEL.+852 2555 2202
18 Kau U Fong, Central
中环九如坊18号
www.thechairmangroup.com

⬚ ◑⬚

🍴○

THE CHAIRMAN
大班楼

The Chairman looks to small suppliers and local fishermen for its ingredients and much of the produce used is also organic. Showing respect for the provenance of ingredients, and using them in homemade sauces and flavoursome dishes such as steamed crab with aged Shaoxing, crispy chicken stuffed with shrimp paste and almond sweet soup, has attracted a loyal following. The restaurant is divided into four different sections and service is pleasant and reassuringly experienced.

大班楼的食材来自小型供应商和本地渔民，大部分都是有机材料，且将精挑细选的材料用来制作酱料和烹调美味菜式，如鸡油花雕蒸大花蟹、香煎百花鸡件配鱼露、生磨杏仁茶等，吸引不少忠实顾客。餐厅分成四个不同用餐区，服务令人宾至如归。

Michelin

THE SQUARE
翠玉轩

To retain the food's natural flavour, the chef insists on using fresh, seasonal produce – he also cooks in a healthy way. Delicacies such as poached spotted garoupa in soya milk broth, and crispy fried boneless chicken stuffed with minced prawn purée are worth a try. Climbing the small staircase up to The Square always adds to the sense of anticipation and this is all the greater these days as the last makeover left the room looking very handsome.

每次踏上往翠玉轩的梯级，内心总会惦念着其美味佳肴和贴心服务，不期然便加快了步伐。这儿的粤菜烹调甚具心思，大厨选用時令食材，加上细腻健康的烹调方式，保留并突出了食材原味。美食包括鲜豆浆浸海星石斑及脆皮江南百花鸡等。

HONG KONG
香港

TEL.+852 2525 1163
Shop 401, 4F, Exchange Square Podium, Central
中环交易广场平台4楼401号铺
www.maxims.com.hk

ASIA 亚洲

The Square

TIM'S KITCHEN (SHEUNG WAN)
桃花源小厨（上环）

Success lead to Tim's Kitchen moving to these premises in 2010 – it's in the same area as before but, with two floors and a capacity of 100, is much larger; chef-owner Tim's son designed the colourful, modern room. Plenty of choice is offered, including popular specialities like Crystal prawn, pomelo skin and pork stomach, which showcase the kitchen's respect for the ingredients.

桃花源小厨迁至现址后，共有两层，可容纳一百人。店主兼厨师黎先生的儿子设计了色彩丰富兼时尚的房间。新店比旧店提供更多粤菜，当然，镇店菜如玻璃虾球、柚皮及猪肚仍然罗列在菜单上，每款食品都证明厨房对优质材料的高度重视。

TEL.+852 2543 5919
84-90 Bonham Strand, Sheung Wan
上环文咸东街84-90号
www.timskitchen.com.hk

ASIA 亚洲

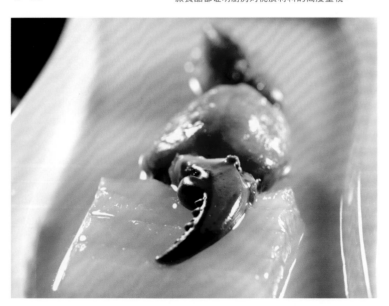

Tim's Kitchen

TSUI HANG VILLAGE
(TSIM SHA TSUI)
翠亨邨（尖沙咀）

Many in Tsim Sha Tsui will recognise the name, as Tsui Hang Village opened in this shopping mall in the 1970s, before moving upstairs in 2011 into more contemporary surroundings. The menu is largely traditional Cantonese, supplemented by the head chef's own creations. Through the large window watch the chefs prepare specialities like braised beef ribs, shredded chicken and honey-glazed barbecued pork – their best seller; the dim sum is also good.

尖沙咀坊众大都会认识翠亨邨，因为它早在1970年代已经在这个购物商场开业。菜式以传统粤菜为主，再加上一些大厨自家创作。透过大玻璃窗，你可以看到厨师烹调各式佳肴，如酱烧牛肋排、翠亨邨靓一鸡及最畅销的蜜汁叉烧；这儿的点心也非常出色。

HONG KONG
香港

TEL.+852 2376 2882

Shop 507, 5F, Mira Place 1, 132 Nathan Road, Tsim Sha Tsui

尖沙咀弥敦道132号
美丽华广场一期5楼507号铺

www.miradining.com

♿ ⟷ 🅿 ☕🍴

ASIA 亚洲

Tsui Hang Village

HONG KONG
香港

TEL.+852 3983 0688

2F, Crowne Plaza Kowloon East, 3 Tong Tak Street, Tseung Kwan O

将军澳唐德街3号
香港九龙东皇冠假日酒店2楼

www.crowneplaza.com/ kowlooneast

🍴

TZE YUET HEEN
紫粵軒

The main restaurant of the Crowne Plaza Kowloon East hotel is this smart Cantonese restaurant. It uses a water theme as the inspiration behind its design and its painted screens and artwork are brought to life by judicious lighting. Over 100 Cantonese dishes are on offer, including plenty of vegetarian options and healthy delicacies, and preparation methods are largely traditional. The set menus are particularly appealing.

紫粵軒提供过百款依照传统烹调方法炮制的广东菜，还有一系列美味健康素菜。选择午、晚市套餐，可一次过品尝多款厨师推介。装潢以流水作主题，融入中国传统绘画艺术：涓涓流水般的地毯、半透明水墨画屏风和独特的天花灯饰等，均显示出设计者的巧思。

Tze Yuet Heen

YIN YUE
殷悦

Yin Yue provides a warm and relaxing space; its large windows letting in lots of light and providing great views of Tsuen Wan from its perch on the top floor of a hotel. The cooking is undertaken by an experienced chef who prepares the attractively presented dishes in a traditional but healthy way, using secret recipes, quality ingredients and a lesser amount of oil. Try suckling pig with dried mullet roe, or stir-fried beef with black truffle.

位于酒店顶楼，以淡色系作装潢的餐厅，格调轻松。两边的落地玻璃窗除了引入自然光外，还让你一览旧社区的景色。店内粤菜由富数十年经验大厨主理，结合了健康少油的烹调方式与传统秘方，再配上世界各地食材和日本美学，形味俱佳。推介菜式有用台湾乌鱼子制作的乌金麒麟乳猪和黑松露牛柳粒。

HONG KONG
香港

TEL.+852 2409 3182
30F, Panda Hotel, 3 Tsuen Wah Street, Tsuen Wan
荃湾荃华街3号悦来酒店30楼
www.pandahotel.com.hk/en/dining/yinyue

ASIA 亚洲

Yin Yue

YUÈ (GOLD COAST)
粤（黄金海岸）

It's not often one can enjoy Cantonese food surrounded by verdant scenery but here on the ground floor of the Gold Coast hotel that's exactly what you get as this comfortable restaurant looks out onto a delightful garden. The menu includes both traditional and more contemporary dishes and it's worth seeking out the chef's specialities such as barbecued pork and chicken liver with honey, and deep-fried chicken with shrimp paste.

HONG KONG
香港

TEL.+852 2452 8668

LG, Gold Coast Hotel, 1 Castle Peak Road, Gold Coast
黄金海岸青山公路1号
黄金海岸酒店低层
www.goldcoasthotel.com.hk

位于黄金海岸酒店的地面层，优雅舒适的室内环境，与落地玻璃窗外的园林景致巧妙地配合起来。选择丰富的餐单提供传统怀旧及较创新的粤菜，厨师精选菜式如蜜饯金钱鸡和星洲虾酱炸鸡件等，值得一试。边品尝美味的广式点心边欣赏怡人的园林美景，实在是赏心乐事。

Yann Chambrier/Yuè

156

ЇѺ

YUÈ (NORTH POINT)
粤（北角）

It may seem like nothing more than a mezzanine area of the City Garden hotel but it's well worth coming up here for the Cantonese food. The experienced chef's respect for the traditions of Cantonese cuisine is clearly demonstrated in dishes like double-boiled jus of almonds with fish maw, fried rice with prawns and barbecue pork, and seared garoupa with layered egg white. There are a number of different sized private rooms.

看起来只是城市花园酒店的间层，并不特别，定让不少人忽略了这间中菜厅，但绝对值得前来一尝这儿的粤菜。资深大厨对传统粤菜的尊重完全反映在其制作的各样菜式上，例如杏汁花胶炖蹄筋、师傅炒饭和雪岭红梅映松露等。餐厅设有不同大小的厢房供各类宴会之用。

HONG KONG
香港

TEL.+852 2806 4918

1F, City Garden Hotel, 9 City Garden Road, North Point
北角城市花园道9号城市花园酒店1楼

www.citygarden.com.hk

&. ⇄ 🛏 🅿 ☺️

ASIA 亚洲

Yuè

MACAU
澳门

✿ ✿ ✿

THE EIGHT
8餐厅

The lavish interior uses the traditional Chinese elements of the goldfish and the number eight to ensure good fortune for all who dine here. The cuisine is a mix of Cantonese and Huaiyang, but the kitchen also adds its own innovative touches to some dishes. Specialities include steamed crab claw with ginger and Chinese wine, and stir-fried lobster with egg, minced pork and black bean. At lunchtime, over 40 kinds of dim sum are served.

豪华的内部装潢采用了传统中国元素，如金鱼及数目字八，寓意所有到访的客人都会遇上好运。菜式融合了广东及淮扬风味，部分美食更渗入了创新点子。推介菜式有姜米酒蒸鲜蟹钳及广东式炒龙虾。午餐时段供应逾四十款点心。

MACAU
澳门

TEL.+853 8803 7788

2F, Grand Lisboa Hotel, Avenida de Lisboa
葡京路新葡京酒店2楼
www.grandlisboahotel.com

GOLDEN FLOWER
京花轩

Within the Encore hotel is this elegant and sophisticated restaurant, whose kitchen is noted for its dextrous use of superb ingredients in the preparation of three different cuisines: Sichuan, Lu and Tan – along with a few Cantonese dishes. The room is adorned with the colours of gold and orange and the booths are the prized seats, but wherever you sit you'll receive charming service from the strikingly attired ladies, including the 'tea sommelier'.

京花轩坐落于澳门万利酒店内,以金色和橙色装潢,既典雅又独特。店内设有圆形白色皮卡座,不管安坐何处,都能享受端庄的女侍应的悉心服务,包括"调茶"服务。厨房最出色之处,除了选料上乘,还能俐落地烹调出川菜、鲁菜、谭家菜三款不同菜系的菜式,同时供应少量广东菜。

MACAU
澳门

TEL.+853 8986 3663

GF, Encore Hotel, Rua Cidade de Sintra, Nape
外港新填海区仙德丽街万利酒店地下

www.wynnmacau.com

Golden Flower

❁ ❁

JADE DRAGON
誉珑轩

Traditional Chinese art, ebony, crystal, gold and silver converge with modern design to form this stunning and eminently comfortable Cantonese restaurant. Equal thought has gone into the details, such as the striking carved jade chopstick holder. The specialities to look out for are goose grilled over lychee wood, and barbecued Ibérico pork. Seafood is also a highlight, along with herbal soups and recipes based on traditional medicine.

誉珑轩的瑰丽装潢十分美轮美奂。乌木、金、银和水晶的运用，揉合了现代设计与中国传统美学的精髓，透明方柱酒窖、豪华厢房，或是餐桌上的玉雕筷子座，都给人留下深刻印象。食材均是高级用料。按中药处方熬煮的老火汤和以荔枝柴烤制的烧鹅和黑毛猪叉烧值得一试。

MACAU
澳门

TEL.+853 8868 2822

Level 2, The Shops at the Boulevard, City of Dreams, Estrada do Istmo, Cotai

路氹连贯公路新濠天地新濠大道2楼

www.cityofdreamsmacau.com/en/dining

❀ ⇄ ◐¶

ASIA 亚洲

David Hartung/Jade Dragon

MACAU
澳门

TEL.+853 2875 7218

G05-07, GF, AIA Tower, 251A-301 Avenida Comercial de Macau

澳门商业大马路友邦广场地下 G05-07

KING
帝皇楼

Though discreetly tucked away in a commercial building, it hasn't stopped the regulars coming for their Cantonese dishes. The signature dishes include braised abalone with goose web, and baked chicken with Shaoxing wine; the homemade dim sum also comes highly recommended. Being sufficiently removed from the casinos means the atmosphere is comparatively sedate.

这家隐藏在商业大楼内的餐厅并不显眼，但却有不少捧场熟客。此酒家的招牌菜有鹅掌扣吉品鲍鱼及花雕焗飞天鸡，自制点心亦十分值得一试。酒家位置与各大赌场之间有一段距离，环境较为宁静。

LAI HEEN
丽轩

If you're looking to impress then you can't fail with this Cantonese restaurant on the top floor of the Ritz-Carlton hotel. The stunning room is richly decorated and supremely comfortable, as are the numerous private dining rooms which can be opened out and enlarged. The ambition of the kitchen is apparent in the Cantonese specialities – they are presented in a modern way and are a match for the sumptuous surroundings.

丽轩位处丽思卡尔顿酒店51楼，居高临下，尽赏窗外秀丽景色。富丽堂皇的装潢与造型时尚精致的传统粤菜，同时满足视觉与味觉的需求。馆内设有五间装饰同样华美，能随时将木板墙移开腾出更多空间的私人厢房，适合举行大小宴会。

MACAU
澳门

TEL.+853 8886 6742

51F, The Ritz-Carlton, Galaxy, Estrada da Baia da N. Senhora da Esperanca, Cotai

氹仔路望德圣母湾大马路银河综合渡假城丽思卡尔顿酒店51楼

www.ritzcarlton.com/macau

Lai Heen

PEARL DRAGON
玥龙轩

No expense has been spared at this elegant and luxurious Cantonese restaurant on the 2nd floor of Studio City. The menu offers a range of refined Cantonese dishes: soy-braised dishes from the lychee wood barbecue are a speciality. Other highlights are double-boiled chicken soup with matsutake and sea conch; stir-fried lobster with caviar; and seafood rice with fish maw and sea cucumber. The tea counter offers a choice of over 50 premium teas.

这家位于新濠影汇酒店的粤菜餐厅装潢素雅，但细节中显心思。香茗选择逾五十款，酒柜内放满陈年佳酿，餐桌上的雕塑、餐具和转盘皆是著名品牌出品，雍雅豪华。餐单选择繁多，招牌菜包括果木烧烤和卤水菜式，油泡龙虾球伴黑鱼子和上品海皇泡饭均值得一试。贴心周到的服务，令用餐过程更添美满。

ASIA 亚洲

MACAU
澳门

TEL.+853 8865 6560

Shop 2111, Level 2, Star Tower, Studio City Hotel, Estrada do Istmo, The Cotai Strip, Taipa
路氹连贯公路新濠影汇酒店巨星汇2楼2111号
www.studiocity-macau.com

TIM'S KITCHEN
桃花源小厨

Hong Kong foodies make special pilgrimages here and it's easy to see why: the Cantonese dishes may appear quite simple but they are very skilfully prepared. Among the highlights are poached and sliced pork stomach in wasabi sauce, and sweet & sour pork ribs. Do make sure you try the crystal prawn and, during the winter, the tasty snake ragout. The restaurant is decorated with a variety of operatic costumes and photos.

香港食家喜欢专程到此朝圣,原因十分简单:此食店的广东菜式看似简单,却实在是经过精心巧手炮制。推介菜式包括凉拌爽肚片及京都骨。此外,万勿错过玻璃虾球,而冬天的重点推介则离不开美味的蛇羹。餐厅放满戏曲照片和戏服装饰,散发出淡淡的艺术气息。

MACAU
澳门

TEL.+853 8803 3682
Shop F25, GF, Hotel Lisboa, East Wing, 2-4 Avenida de Lisboa
葡京路2-4号葡京酒店东翼地下F25号铺
www.hotelisboa.com

ASIA 亚洲

Tim's Kitchen

WING LEI
永利轩

The bright yellow look gives the room an airy feel, while the tassel lamps hanging from the ceiling cast a romantic glow. The centrepiece of the room, however, remains the three-dimensional flying dragon made up of 100,000 sparkling Swarovski crystals. At lunch over 40 dim sum are available, while the à la carte offers a great range of refined Cantonese classics. The 'Signature Menu' is a good way of trying the chef's best dishes.

明亮的黄色装潢营造出轻松悠闲的气氛，大型灯笼透出浪漫灯光，衬托以十万片水晶制成的立体飞龙，尽展豪华气派；舒适宽敞的座椅让人生出好感。餐厅装潢一流，服务也亲切周到。传统粤菜，菜式选择良多，大厨精髓菜谱是一尝其手艺的最佳选择。午市的手工点心叫人眼花撩乱，不妨点选自选点心套餐。

MACAU
澳门

TEL.+853 8986 3663

GF, Wynn Hotel, Rua Cidade de Sintra, Nape
外港新填海区仙德丽街永利酒店地下

www.wynnmacau.com

ASIA 亚洲

www.dadokit.com/Wing Lei

YING
帝影楼

It's not just the breathtaking views looking north to Macau that set this restaurant apart – the beautifully styled interior has been designed with taste and verve; the beaded curtains, which feature gold cranes and crystal trees, are particularly striking. The Cantonese dishes are prepared with contemporary twists and much flair. Try the deep-fried crispy chicken with lemon sauce, and lobster Cantonese style.

帝影楼北望海港及澳门繁华景色，环境宜人。餐厅设计品味独特，风格绚丽；珠帘上饰有金鹤和水晶树图案，使装潢更添神采。餐厅的粤菜融入了新口味，大厨的烹调技艺精湛。专业的服务态度令人宾至如归。值得一试的有柠香脆皮鸡和粤式炒龙虾。

MACAU
澳门

TEL.+853 2886 8868
11F, Altira Hotel, Avenida de Kwong Tung, Taipa
氹仔广东大马路新濠锋酒店11楼
www.altiramacau.com/en/dining/detail/15/ying

David Hartung/Ying

ZI YAT HEEN
紫逸轩

With a large glass-enclosed wine cellar at its centre, Zi Yat Heen is an elegant yet intimate restaurant, located within the Four Seasons Hotel Macau. By using first rate ingredients and minimal amounts of seasoning, chef Ho prepares a traditional Cantonese menu but one that is lighter and fresher tasting. Interesting creations include the baked lamb chops with coffee sauce, while a more traditional dish would be pigeon with Yunnan ham.

地方宽敞，格调高雅的紫逸轩位于四季酒店一楼，正中位置设有巨型玻璃餐酒库。厨师烹调传统菜式时采用最新鲜的食材与最少的调味料，炮制出更鲜味清新的粤菜。有趣创意菜式包括咖啡汁焗羊排，较传统的选择有酥香云腿伴鸽脯。

MACAU
澳门

TEL.+853 2881 8888

GF, Four Seasons Hotel, Estrada da Baia de N. Senhora da Esperanca, s/n, The Cotai Strip, Taipa
氹仔路氹金光大道望德圣母湾大马路四季酒店地下

www.fourseasons.com/macau

🕸 ♿ 🔛 🍽 🅿

Cristiano Nantes/Zi Yat Heen

CHAN SENG KEI
陈胜记

Chan Seng Kei has stood next to the ancient church for over 70 years and is now run by the 3rd generation of the family. It's well known for its traditional Cantonese food, with seafood supplied daily by the local fishermen. The signature dish is Stewed duck with tangerine peel but, as the cooking process takes more than 10 hours, only a few are available each day. It's a simple, semi open-air restaurant intertwined with several old banyan trees.

坐落旧教堂旁的陈胜记开业至今已传至第三代,向以传统粤菜和海鲜菜式驰名。新鲜野生海鲜每天直接从渔民处采购;而制作工序繁复,需烹调十个小时的陈皮鸭是其招牌菜,每天限量供应。半开放式餐室非常朴实,当中数棵树身粗壮的老榕树,见证着饭店逾七十载历史。

MACAU
澳门

TEL.+853 2888 2021
21 Rua Caetano, Coloane
路环计单奴街21号

ASIA 亚洲

HOU KONG CHI KEI
濠江志记美食

There are a couple of challenges to overcome – it'll take you a while to find this hidden little shop and the environment is not particularly striking – but the satisfying Cantonese dishes, which reflect owner-chef Mr. Chan's great enthusiasim for food, are well worth coming for. Call in advance to reserve the fresh seafood dishes like the steamed crab with sticky rice; also try the barbecued fish and the deep-fried taro fish ball.

要找到这家位置隐蔽的餐厅确是个小小的挑战，其环境亦非十分出众；但你所获得的回报，就是一尝东主兼厨师陈先生主理的广式佳肴，并感受他对烹调美食的热情。个别海鲜美食如蒸糯米蟹饭，需致电预订；其他推介菜式还有烧鱼及香芋炸鱼球。

MACAU
澳门

TEL.+853 2895 3098

GF, Block 3, Lai Hou Gardens, Rua Coelho do Amaral

白鸽巢前地丽豪花园第三座地铺佳乐园石级上

Michelin

LOU KEI (FAI CHI KEI)
老记（筷子基）

If you're looking for a simple, good value supper then Lou Kei may well fit the bill. Granted, it may not be in the centre of town, but every cab driver knows this lively place. It has been renowned for over 20 years for its sizeable selection of tasty noodles, congee and Cantonese dishes; frogs' legs in a clay pot and sea crab congee are both highly recommended. The interior is bright and neat while the service is polite and attentive.

若然你想品尝廉物美的美食，老记便是不二之选。尽管餐厅并非位于市中心，但是所有的士司机皆知这间驰名食府的位置。老记二十多年来提供美味粥品面食及广东菜式，其田鸡腿煲及水蟹粥更备受食客推崇，店内明亮洁净，侍应亲切有礼。

MACAU
澳门

TEL.+853 2856 9494

Avenida Da Concórdia N, 12R/C E S/L Loja H
和乐大马路12号宏基大厦第4座H及M铺

⌐s⌐

ASIA 亚洲

Michelin

TOU TOU KOI
陶陶居

As this 80 year old restaurant is always packed, it's vital to book ahead; at the same time why not also pre-order the duck? It's dim sum during the day and Cantonese cuisine at night and among the favourites are deep-fried crab, deep-fried US beef belly and fish from the tank in the dining room. Service is sufficiently swift to accommodate the non-stop flow of customers. A refurbishment has left the restaurant looking much more contemporary.

有八十多年历史的陶陶居总是宾客如云，必须订座，你亦可顺道预订八宝鸭。日间以点心为主，晚上则提供粤菜，受欢迎菜式包括金钱蟹盒和脆皮美国牛坑腩，还有新鲜烹调的海鱼。为了应付络绎不绝的客人，侍应生的工作效率十分高。早上九时开始有早茶供应，吸引不少茶客前来一聚。

MACAU
澳门

TEL.+853 2857 2629
6-8 Travessa do Mastro
炉石塘巷6-8号

Tou Tou Koi

BI YING
碧迎居

The name means 'sure win' and it provides the ideal pit-stop if you need a quick break from the gaming tables. It's a busy 24-hour operation with its focus on the open kitchen where you can watch noodles being made. The menu offers a culinary journey around China, with plenty of regional specialties, although the wood-roasted dishes are a particular highlight. Finish with one of the desserts made with medicinal herbs.

位处酒店娱乐场所旁的碧迎居,二十四小时提供大江南北美馔,不论你钟情川式脆椒炒肉蟹、佛跳墙、古法酱烧琵琶鸭,或巧手南北点心,都能尽情满足口欲。不妨试试其招牌烧味,以灵芝龟灵膏或花旗参冰糖炖官燕作结也不错。开放式厨房设有果木烧烤炉,食客更有机会观赏手拉面条的制作过程。

MACAU
澳门

TEL.+853 8865 6650
Shop 1182, Level 1 Casino at Studio City Hotel, Estrada do Istmo, Cotai
路氹连贯公路新濠影汇娱乐场1楼1182号铺
www.studiocity-macau.com

CANTON

喜粤

Modern in design and colored in a deep sensual red, Canton is a stylish restaurant with a sophisticated atmosphere – and is hidden away in a corner of the world's biggest indoor gaming floor. A Kouan-Chiau (gastronomic) version of Cantonese cooking is provided, with dishes like Steamed egg white topped with red birds nest, and Deep-fried duck with almond flake in a lime sauce. Popular Sichuan dishes are also available.

喜粤位于全球最大室内娱乐场的一角，采用诱人的深红色作主调，装潢时尚。菜单以广州粤菜如太极芙蓉红燕及西柠杏香鸭片等为主。此外，店内亦有提供数款四川名菜，让食客有更多美食选择。

MACAU
澳门

TEL.+853 8118 9930

Shop 1018, Casino level, The Venetian Resort, Estrada da Baia de N. Senhora da Esperanca, s/n, The Cotai Strip, Taipa

氹仔路氹金光大道-望德圣母湾大马路威尼斯人酒店娱乐场地下1018号铺

www.venetianmacao.com/restaurants/signature/canton.html

Canton

DYNASTY 8
朝

Old China is celebrated at this sophisticated and professionally run Chinese restaurant within the Conrad hotel. It takes its name and decorative styling from the eight dynasties of ancient China – Qin, Han, Sui, Tang, Song, Yuan, Ming and Qing – which are also used as the names of the private dining rooms. The traditional Cantonese food includes a varied choice of dim sum at lunch and the restaurant boasts an impressive wine cellar.

朝，顾名思义，其名字和室内装潢意念源自中国古代八个皇朝：秦、汉、隋、唐、宋、元、明、清。雕花木椅、木地板、红灯笼和中式古典檐篷带来强烈的中国古风。此店除供应以最新鲜的食材制作的传统广东小菜外，午市亦有点心供应，还设有酒窖，适合爱酒人士。

MACAU
澳门

TEL.+853 8113 8920

Level 1, Conrad Hotel, Estrada do Istmo, s/n, Cotai
路氹连贯公路康莱德酒店1楼
www.sandscotaicentral.com/ restaurants/chinese/dynasty-8.html

MACAU
澳门

TEL.+853 8886 2182

Shop 2008, 2F, Galaxy Macau, Coloane-Taipa

路氹城澳门银河综合渡假城2楼
2008号铺

www.fooklammoon-grp.com

FOOK LAM MOON
福临门

One of the most famous restaurant names in Hong Kong has long been celebrated for its traditional Cantonese menu. It is also known for its clientele of high-rollers and decision makers, so it was perhaps inevitable that a branch would eventually appear in Macau. You'll find local lobster on the menu, along with their famous crispy chicken; many regulars opt for the chicken stuffed with bird's nest – even though it isn't always listed on the menu.

门外悬挂着的一副对联和椭圆形的水晶吊灯为餐厅营造了别具一格的气派。福临门是香港享负盛名的粤菜酒家,熟客都懂得预订餐牌上没有的凤吞燕,当红炸子鸡则是厨师得意之作,此外,选用本地BB龙虾制作的油泡龙虾球亦值得一试。食客更可向驻场的专业品酒师请教搭配美酒佳肴的心得。

IMPERIAL COURT
金殿堂

A massive marble pillar with a carved dragon dominates this elegant and contemporary restaurant, which is found on the same floor as the VIP lobby. The kitchen prepares classic Cantonese cuisine, with dishes such as scrambled organic egg whites with sea urchin and crabmeat, which is topped with caviar; braised boneless pork knuckle; and turtle rim in shrimp roe sauce. The impressive wine list includes over 2,000 labels.

金殿堂与贵宾大堂位于同一楼层，庞大的雕龙云石柱是最瞩目之处，设计风格高贵优雅中见时尚。餐厅主要供应广东美食，如海胆鲜蟹肉炒蛋白及虾子瑞裙边扣猪肘等；餐酒选择逾千种，令人印象深刻。

MACAU
澳门

TEL.+853 8802 2361

GF, MGM Hotel, Avenida Dr. Sun Yat Sen, Nape

外港新填海区孙逸仙大马路美高梅酒店地下

www.mgm.mo

¶O

KAM LAI HEEN
金丽轩

Grand Lapa's Cantonese restaurant is an elegant space, with eye-catching ceiling lights and subtle Chinese design motifs. The longstanding chef and his team prepare traditional Cantonese cuisine which goes down well with their many local Macanese customers. Signature dishes include steamed silver cod in Oolong tea soup, and scallops and soft bean curd soup; it is also worth pre-ordering the Beggar's chicken.

金丽轩位于酒店大堂之上，装潢并非十分豪华，却有一种自然的宁静与优雅。经验十足的厨师团队按传统技法，炮制一系列富澳门特色的粤菜。冻顶银鳕鱼及茶壶豆腐海鲜汤均值得尝试。

MACAU
澳门

TEL.+853 8793 3821

1F, Grand Lapa Hotel, 956-1110
Avenida da Amizade, Macau

澳门友谊大马路956-1110号金丽
华酒店1楼

www.grandlapa.com

& ⇔ P ⓞ¶

Kam Lai Heen

LEI GARDEN
利苑酒家

A smart restaurant set amongst the canals of this vast hotel's third floor – arrive by gondola if you wish... Venetian guests predominate here; gamblers mostly give it a miss as it's too far from the gaming tables. Walls of marble provide the backdrop to a comprehensive range of traditional Cantonese dishes which are delivered by an efficient and well-organised team of servers. The best place to be seated is in one of the cosy booths.

餐厅设于三楼,占据此大型酒店运河旁的位置,雄据地利,顾客可以乘坐贡朵拉前往这儿。由于离赌场较远,娱乐场玩家通常会光顾其他餐厅,因此这里的顾客以酒店住客为主。云石墙壁与传统广东菜互相映衬。服务效率非常高。最好的座位是靠近前门的舒适卡位。

MACAU
澳门

TEL.+853 2882 8689

Shop 855, 3F Grand Canal Shoppes, The Venetian Resort, Estrada da Baia de N. Senhora de Esperança, Taipa

氹仔路望德圣母湾大马路威尼斯人酒店大运河购物中心3楼855号铺

www.venetianmacao.com

Lei Garden

🍴○

LUNG WAH TEA HOUSE
龙华茶楼

ASIA 亚洲

MACAU
澳门

TEL.+853 2857 4456

3 Rua Norte do Mercado Aim-Lacerda
提督市北街3号

🚫🍴 ⑤

Little has changed from when this old-style Cantonese tea house, up a flight of stairs, opened in the 1960s: the large clock still works, the boss still uses an abacus to add the bill and you still have to refill your own pot of tea at the boiler. The owner buys fresh produce, including chicken for their most popular dish, from the market across the road; stir-fried noodles with beef is another speciality. Get here early for the fresh dim sum.

这家有一列楼梯的传统广东茶楼自1960年代开业以来，变化不大——古老大钟依然在摆动，店东依然用算盘结算帐单，你依然要自行到热水器前冲茶。店主从对面街市选购新鲜食材烹调美食，包括茶楼名菜油鸡。建议早上前来享用新鲜点心。

Michelin

180

SAN TOU TOU
新陶陶

Found on a narrow street in the centre of Taipa is this Cantonese restaurant, run by the same family for three generations and now supervised by two brothers. The cooking is very traditional and it is the chicken soup served in very hot clay pots that attracts so many; but there are plenty of other, more affordable, specialities. The restaurant is spread over two floors and the air conditioning is the most efficient!

这间家族经营的广东菜餐厅位于氹仔中心地带的小巷内，现时由第三代的两兄弟主理。煮法非常传统，炖鸡汤用砂锅盛载，吸引大量食客。除此之外，这里还提供很多价钱相宜的小菜选择。

MACAU
澳门

TEL.+853 2882 7065
26 Rua Correia da Silva, Taipa
氹仔告利雅施利华街26号

SHANGHAI
上海

‡‡ ‡‡

CANTON 8 (RUNAN STREET)
喜粤8号（汝南街）

This is the place to go for quality dim sum and classic Cantonese fare at affordable prices. The head chef has over 50 years of experience in Cantonese cooking. The menu is not overly long but is updated regularly, showcasing the quintessence of the cuisine alongside newer dishes. Apart from double-steamed soups, roast meats, stir-fries and a myriad of fish dishes, the desserts are also unmissable.

店东林先生富多年餐厅运营经验，开店的目标非常清晰：让食客以亲民的价格品尝到高素质的广东点心和小菜。在厨房领军的简师傅掌厨逾五十年，经验丰富，更不时花心思更新菜单，以求为客人带来新鲜感。餐单菜式不多却简而精，除了炖汤、烧味、小炒和五花八门的鱼类菜式，甜点更是不容错过。

SHANGHAI
上海

TEL.+86 21 6733 7123
63 Runan Street, Huangpu
黄浦区汝南街63号

❀❀

IMPERIAL TREASURE
御宝轩

The Imperial Treasure Group from Singapore has a diverse catering portfolio – this restaurant of theirs at Yi Feng Galleria focuses on Cantonese cuisine. The dining room, a worthy match for the food, is elegantly dressed with plenty of crystal. The kitchen prepares the cuisine in a traditional style, whether that's something simple like wonton noodles or dishes that require much more preparation such as crispy chicken with glutinous rice.

来自新加坡的御宝集团餐饮种类多元化，设于益丰·外滩源的这家提供各式高级粤菜，如海鲜、汤品、烧味和点心，食物水准上乘，不论是功夫菜如糯米炸子鸡或简单的云吞面，均做得正宗而精细，尽显厨师手艺。建议订座时预留大热的炖汤和烧味。环境同样一丝不苟，餐室以黑色作主调，配以大量水晶，格调优雅。

SHANGHAI
上海

TEL.+86 21 5308 1188

4F, Yi Feng Galleria, 99 East Beijing Road, Huangpu
黄浦区北京东路99号
益丰·外滩源4楼

☐ 🅿 ◐🍴

Imperial Treasure

T'ANG COURT
唐阁

After passing along the gorgeous curved corridor of private rooms, you may feel that the main dining room, with just six formally dressed tables, is a little understated. However, the charm and professionalism of the staff will soon put you at ease. The newly joined chef delivers a mix of classic and modern Cantonese dishes. Specialities include braised red lobster with sea urchin and braised fish maw with crab roe. Private rooms serve a set menu only.

盘旋曲折的走廊上，布满私人厢房；主餐室只有六张布置得一丝不苟的餐桌。专业的服务团队配合高素质的食物，让用餐成为美妙愉快的经历！餐单上是经典与现代风味融合而成的粤菜，令人印象深刻。新加入的厨师团队为餐厅带来新气象，白雪藏金龙和脆百合炒和牛粒都是其得意之作。包厢只供应套餐。

SHANGHAI
上海

TEL.+86 21 2330 2288

5F, The Langham, 99 Madang Road, Xintiandi, Huangpu
黄浦区新天地马当路99号
朗廷酒店5楼
www.xintiandi.langhamhotels.com

YI LONG COURT
逸龙阁

The Peninsula hotel's flagship restaurant provides luxurious dining in an elegant, urbane space inspired by 1930s Shanghai. The menu of Cantonese classics is prepared by a chef with many years of experience in Hong Kong – one of the dishes to go for is the barbecued iberico pork. The individually furnished private rooms are beautiful to behold; and to fully experience the culinary craft here, consider booking the Chef's Table.

半岛酒店旗下的旗舰粤菜餐馆，装潢布置以1930年代上海菜馆的风格为骨干，将典雅、细致与奢华融合于一。由富多年经验的香港主厨设计的菜单内全是经典粤菜，不妨试试黑豚肉叉烧及煎焗沙姜乳鸽脯。私人厢房布置得美仑美奂，甚有旧上海靡丽之风。

SHANGHAI
上海

TEL.+86 21 2327 2888

2F, The Peninsula Hotel, Bund 32, 32 Zhongshan Dong Yi Road , Huangpu
黄浦区中山东一路32号外滩32号
半岛酒店2楼
www.peninsula.com/shanghai

AMAZING CHINESE CUISINE
菁禧荟

You'll need to plan ahead a little if you want to enjoy the Chao Zhou cuisine here at Amazing Chinese Cuisine. Making a booking is the first challenge as it only has five private rooms. Secondly, customers are encouraged to pre-order otherwise they'll find many of the menu's dishes are not available. Consider going for the marinated goose head; chilled crab Chao Zhou style; or seasonal offerings like marinated mantis shrimps.

菁禧荟的地址实为一幢别墅，店内没有主餐室，只有五个房间，因此，预订座位是必须的，同时，为了确保能吃上喜欢的菜式，也必须要预订菜式。高级潮州菜如潮州卤水老鹅头，花了三年时间酿制，还有鲜甜多膏的潮式冻花蟹，全都不能错过。潮式生腌红膏富贵虾只有在时令季节才供应。此店设有最低消费额。

SHANGHAI
上海

TEL.+86 21 6262 5677
B5 Villa, 1665 Hongqiao Road, Changning
长宁区虹桥路1665号B5别墅

JI PIN COURT
吉品轩

Remodelled from a heritage building in the former French Concession, this is a serene oasis amid the busy city centre. Chef Cheung has over 20 years of experience in Cantonese cooking and he is keen to imbue the cuisine with new elements. Attention to detail is clear in his cooking – soups are made with spring water and char siu is glazed in longan honey. Dim sum is served at lunch. Regulars tend to pre-order seafood when reserving.

餐厅位于一幢法式古建筑内，尤如繁嚣闹市中的绿洲。主厨有超过二十年烹调经验，其对传统粤菜的掌握毋庸置疑，难得是他仍致力推陈出新研发菜式。其招牌菜包括以特选矿泉水炖煮五至六小时的炖汤及用龙眼蜜制作的叉烧；还有流心富贵虾等海鲜菜式。餐厅设多款一人分量菜式及套餐。如欲一尝海鲜，建议订座时先作查询。

SHANGHAI
上海

TEL.+86 21 6469 9969

3F, 55 South Wulumuqi Road, Xuhui
徐汇区乌鲁木齐南路55号3楼

Ji Pin Court

LEI GARDEN (PUDONG)
利苑（浦东新区）

Reservations are a must as this Lei Garden in IFC is continuously packed with people craving good quality Cantonese cuisine. At lunchtime, customers come in droves for the expertly crafted dim sum and the soups. The dinner menu offers premium dishes like seafood and dried fish maw. Those wishing to avoid making too much of a dent in their wallets should opt for the seasonal stir-fries and casseroles.

国金中心内的利苑酒家总是座无虚席，概因高素质的粤菜大家都爱吃。老火汤和精制广东点心是午饭时段上班族的最爱。晚饭时间，你可以从主菜单点选海鲜、鱼肚等高级食品，亦可从特别菜单中点选时令小炒或煲仔菜等等。无论中午还是晚上，都必须预早订座。

SHANGHAI
上海

TEL.+86 21 5106 1688

L3-17 & 18, Shanghai IFC Mall, 8 Century Avenue, Pudong

浦东新区世纪大道8号
国金中心商场3楼17-18号

ASIA 亚洲

Lei Garden

LEI GARDEN (XUHUI)
利苑（徐汇）

The chain may be spreading rapidly in Asia but quality control is strictly imposed to ensure all dim sum, roast meats and double-boiled soups remain the same high standard as at the parent restaurant. This branch in a popular mall boasts a hip décor and is always full. 'Crossing-the-bridge' geoduck is blanched at your table in a hot seafood stock that took six hours to make. Claypot rice with preserved meat is made à la minute.

源自香港的利苑集团，业务遍布亚洲各地，提供高素质的正宗粤菜。员工每天都会亲自试菜，监控食材及食品的品质，确保点心、烧味、炖汤维持水准。不妨考虑以每天熬煮超过六小时的海鲜汤即席泡煮的过桥象拔蚌，或是即点即做的腊味煲仔饭。这家位处大型商场的分店装潢时尚，经常满座，建议在订座时同时预留烧味和炖汤等招牌菜。

SHANGHAI
上海

TEL.+86 21 5425 2283

Shop 401, 4F, iapm, 999 Middle Huaihai Road, Xuhui

徐汇区淮海中路999号
环贸广场4楼401号铺

Lei Garden

MADAM GOOSE (MINHANG)
鹅夫人（闵行）

Diners aren't really here for the purple velvet seats and white winged chandeliers – it's the food that keeps them coming back. For its signature roast goose, only 90-day-old birds from Guangdong at a certain weight are used to ensure quality. Other specialities include soy-marinated chicken, swan-shaped char siu pastry, buttered pineapple buns, and fried duck jaws in peppered salt. Roast geese are available in limited quantity so come early.

餐厅装潢别具特色，从布置至食物均以鹅为主题，不能错过的烧鹅选用九十天大、产自广东的黑棕鹅，体重受严密监控，以保持品质，皮脆骨细、肉质嫩滑；由于供应量有限，晚市要尽早前往免扑空。此外，烧味及点心亦别出心裁，当中以菠萝油和天鹅叉烧酥为必试之选。等待出炉烧鹅的同时，不妨来一客椒盐鸭下巴。

SHANGHAI
上海

TEL.+86 21 5470 0508

Shop 422, 4F, The Sky Mall, 5001 Dushi Road, Minhang

闵行区都市路5001号
仲盛世界商城422号

♿ **P** ❚

SHANGHAI
上海

TEL.+86 21 6266 3098

**Unit E2-03, 2F, Tower 1, Jing An
Kerry Centre, 1515 West Nanjing
Road, Jingan**

静安区南京西路1515号
静安嘉里中心1期2楼E2-03

www.seventhson.hk

SEVENTH SON (JINGAN)
家全七福（静安）

After the success of their branch in Pudong, the Hong Kong based group behind these Cantonese restaurants opened this comfortable and traditionally decorated sister in 2014. It also delivers a traditional Cantonese menu, with the technical skills of the chef evident in dishes that range from dried seafood and soups to roast meats and stir-fries. At lunch they offer over 30 varieties of dim sum.

嘉里中心的家全七福于2014年开业，与浦东店同出一脉，熟客都知道这家来自香港的高级粤菜厅背后的故事。这里供应的全是传统功夫粤菜，海味菜式、汤饮、烧味，甚至一碟小炒都是精工细作的佳肴。午市提供逾三十款自家制作的点心。内部装潢贵气中带点怀旧味道。

Seventh Son

XIN RONG JI (HUANGPU)
新荣记（黄浦）

A wall of statues by the entrance demonstrate the effort that has gone into the decoration of this Chinese restaurant, located in a shopping mall opposite a metro station. However, the real attraction is the food. Seafood from Taizhou is the undoubted highlight, but the Cantonese food and the dim sum are carefully prepared. Look out for the sautéed yellow croaker and BBQ pork in a paper bag.

一家位于商场内的中菜厅，地铁站就在对面，位置十分便利。餐室内部环境充满浓烈中国色彩，入口处的一列神像尤为引人注目。然而，吸引人的还有这儿的美味佳肴，主角是台州海鲜，辅以一系列出色的粤菜，午市还有广东点心供应。家烧黄鱼、炖汤和纸包叉烧都是推介菜式。

SHANGHAI
上海

TEL.+86 21 5386 5757

No. 503, 5F, Shanghai Plaza, 138 Middle Huaihai Road, Huangpu

黄浦区淮海中路138号
上海广场5楼503号

www.xinrongji.cc

ASIA 亚洲

Michelin

CRYSTAL JADE (HUANGPU)
翡翠酒家（黄浦）

The Singapore-based group's first restaurant in Shanghai features a strikingly modern interior – ask for one of the prized booths by the window. Many come for a business lunch on weekdays while quite a number of tourists are attracted at night and on weekends. Dim sum is meticulously made by Cantonese chefs – shrimp dumplings and rice noodle rolls are the highlights. Singaporean pepper crab is also worth a try. Booking essential at weekends.

新加坡翡翠集团在上海首家食店，现代装潢中带点中国风，倚窗而设的卡座最受欢迎，餐室中央一张长桌子可让客人拼桌。餐厅颇受上班一族欢迎，但晚上及假日亦不乏慕名而来的游客。叫食客光临的正是其正宗广东美食，其中点心由广东师傅主理，肠粉、虾饺等特别出色。作为新加坡集团，其黑白胡椒炒青蟹亦值得一试。假日宜预早订座。

SHANGHAI
上海

TEL.+86 21 6385 8752

12 A-B, 2F, South Block Xintiandi, 123 Xingye Road, Huangpu

黄浦区兴业路123号
新天地广场南里2楼12 A-B

www.crystaljade.com

ASIA 亚洲

Crystal Jade

FOUR SEASONS
文兴酒家

Its red brick walls, tufted booth seats and solid wood furniture may not fit in the stereotype of a Cantonese restaurant. But its menu is unmistakably Cantonese – meat, veggies and seafood all meticulously roasted, steamed, stir-fried or braised. Try their signature dishes such as the famous crispy duck, and stir-fried lobster with ginger and scallion.

位于晶品购物中心内的文兴酒家，设有小酒吧和户外用餐区，主用餐区以仿古红砖配以木纹地板和木制家具，充满怀旧气息。小厨房内挂满整幅玻璃窗的烧味在提醒你：这是广东菜馆！完备的菜单内全是大家熟悉的粤菜如烧味、蒸煮小菜或小炒、煲仔菜和海鲜等，一应俱全，烧鸭和炒龙虾是其招牌菜。

TEL.+86 21 6287 5001

Shop 605, 6F, Crystal Galleria, 68 Yuyuan Road, Jingan
静安区愚园路68号晶品6楼605

ASIA 亚洲

Four Seasons

SHANGHAI
上海

TEL.+86 21 6330 8217

Room 501, 5F, The Bund Central, 139 East Nanjing Road, Huangpu

黄浦区南京东路139号
外滩中央5楼501室

♿ ⇔ ☺╫

╫○

CANTON 8 (EAST NANJING ROAD)
喜粤8号（南京东路）

The décor befits the heritage of the circa 1930 architecture in the former British Concession. The menu is mostly the same as the Runan Street flagship, but this branch focuses on high-end dishes, such as fried scallops in mashed taro and giant grouper which is shipped in daily. Dim sum is made in-house and soups are double-boiled for at least six hours. Only reservations before 6pm for dinner and 11:30am for lunch are accepted.

餐厅位处一幢建于三十年代并经改建的商场之内，内部装潢充满当时的英式风味。餐牌与汝南路总店有八成相同，但定位更为高档。琳琅满目的菜单上除了即场制作的点心、经六小时炖煮的炖汤，当然亦少不了海鲜菜式，包括每天进货的龙趸。而为保食材新鲜，多数海鲜须预订。餐厅只接受午间十一时半前及晚间六时前的订位。

CRYSTAL JADE (JINGAN)
翡翠酒家（静安）

A shopping mall at West Nanjing Road is home to this bright Cantonese restaurant which benefited from a redecoration in 2015. The chef delivers a classic Cantonese menu that includes roast meats, casseroles, seafood and stir-fried dishes, but he isn't afraid of adding his own innovative touches. As it's under the ownership of a Singapore group, the restaurant also offers some Singaporean specialities like chilli crab.

在熙来攘往的南京西路上逛得倦了，正好到这家粤菜餐厅大快朵颐。餐厅不久前曾进行翻新，在时尚明亮的用餐区用膳格外舒适。来自香港的大厨率领团队炮制一系列粤菜，菜式揉合传统和创新，包括烧味、煲仔菜、海鲜和小炒，同时亦有自制点心供应。由于隶属新加坡集团，故也能尝到新加坡特色菜如辣椒蟹等。

SHANGHAI
上海

TEL.+86 21 5228 1133
Unit 719, 7F, Westgate Mall, 1038
West Nanjing Road, Jingan
静安区南京西路1038号
梅龙镇广场7楼719
www.crystaljade.com

ASIA 亚洲

Crystal Jade

HANG YUEN HIN (PUDONG)
恒悦轩（浦东新区）

This sister to the original branch opened in 2009 and provides a similarly healthy range of carefully prepared Cantonese dishes. It gets particularly busy at lunchtime thanks largely to the quality of the dim sum and soups – these soups, as well as the roast meats, can be pre-ordered when you reserve a table. At dinner, it's dishes like steamed seafood and abalone which prove popular.

恒悦轩在上海市区有两家分店，都是做精致港式粤菜，总厨融汇粤港两地之精髓，选用新鲜时令食材，炮制出少油少盐、保持食材原味又有益健康的菜肴。中午时可以享用港式点心和汤品，晚上可试试清蒸海鲜或金蒜蒸小青龙虾。此店在2009年开业，中午时段颇繁忙，订座时可同时预留食物如例汤和烧味等。

SHANGHAI
上海

TEL.+86 21 6880 9778

3-4F, Standard Chartered Tower, 201 Century Avenue, Pudong

浦东新区世纪大道201号渣打银行大厦3-4楼

!O

HANG YUEN HIN (XUHUI)
恒悦轩（徐汇）

Here at the original Hang Yuen Hin, which opened in 2005, the greenery of the park outside the windows combines with a comfortable dining room to create a relaxing and enjoyable experience. The chef has worked in both Guangzhou and Hong Kong; know-how which he puts to good use in his Cantonese cuisine – his food is also low in salt and oil. Signature dishes include fried shrimp with almond, and double-boiled bird's nest with coconut milk.

SHANGHAI
上海

TEL.+86 21 6472 9778
Xujiahui Park, 290 Wanping Road, Xuhui
徐汇区宛平路290号徐家汇公园内

恒悦轩的总店于2005年在徐家汇公园里开业，舒适的环境加上园林景色，在此用餐确是赏心乐事。餐厅主理高级粤菜，主厨曾于粤港两地工作，融汇两地饮食文化，炮制出少油少盐、保持食材原味又有益健康的菜肴。此店的招牌菜式不少，西杏炸虾卷和木瓜椰奶炖燕窝均值得试试。

JIN XUAN
金轩

The head chef brings the considerable experience he garnered at some famous Cantonese restaurants in Hong Kong to bear at this elegant restaurant on the 53rd floor of the Ritz-Carlton. The wine list is impressive, as is the selection of teas. The views are a given and the room itself is very comfortable and well run.

位于浦东丽思卡尔顿53楼的金轩，由拥有逾十年粤菜经验的厨师主理，以高素质的食材制作出色味皆优的美食。招牌菜包括黄金燕麦龙虾球等。餐厅的一系列茶饮尤为出色。曾是经验侍酒师的餐厅经理可替你搭配餐酒与佳肴。

SHANGHAI
上海

TEL.+86 21 2020 1717

53F, The Ritz-Carlton Pudong, 8 Century Avenue, Pudong

浦东新区世纪大道8号丽思卡尔顿酒店53楼

www.ritzcarlton.com/ shanghaipudong

Jin Xuan

LA SOCIÉTÉ
逸荟

There are a vast number of dining options on Yuanmingyuan Road but if you're after elegantly presented and carefully prepared traditional Cantonese food then this is where to come. The tiny elevator brings you to the 8th floor where the private rooms are located – the main dining room is one level up. The highly experienced team behind this restaurant have put as much attention into the decoration as they have the cooking.

圆明园路上的旧建筑群中开了许多餐厅，逸荟置身于女青年会大楼中，小小的电梯将你带到八楼，这儿全是包厢，上一层便是主餐室，举目尽是黑白二色的大理石，整个空间装饰得华贵优雅。端上桌的粤菜也如室内的装潢般高贵，由点心、烧味、海鲜、海味以至于甜品，都做得细致而风味正宗，看得到店方的心思。

TEL.+86 21 6323 6767

8-9F, Y.W.C.A. Building, Rockbund, 133 Yuanmingyuan Road, Huangpu
黄浦区圆明园路133号洛克·外滩源女青年会大楼8-9楼

ASIA 亚洲

PHAT DUCK
月半鸭

A restaurant specialising in Peking duck. The chef marinates 45-day-old ducks weighing exactly 2.1 kg with puréed celery, ginger, spring onion, garlic and radish before they are roasted to perfection. The barbecue sauce served with the duck is also a secret blend and comes with a hint of curry. As well as cucumber and scallions, prawn crackers and ground peanuts with sugar and sesame are offered as condiments.

月半鸭有"胖鸭"之意，以胖为名概因东主身形比较肥胖，而鸭则当然是指其招牌菜烤鸭。其烤鸭只选用45天大、重四斤二两的北京填鸭，厨师以特别调校的菜汁腌制两小时，以辟走鸭的腥味。烤鸭酱与传统的有所不同，特别加入了咖喱，吃起来更加惹味；鸭片佐以泰国虾片和花生芝麻黄糖也是一大特色。餐厅环境简洁舒适。

SHANGHAI
上海

TEL.+86 21 5241 6602

F57, 2F, Metro Town, 890 Changning Road, Changning

长宁区长宁路890号玫瑰坊2楼F57

P ◑Ⅱ

ASIA 亚洲

Phat Duck

ROYAL CHINA CLUB
皇朝会

Operated by London's Royal China Group, this Cantonese restaurant specialises in dried seafood like abalone and fish, along with other assorted seafood dishes. The quality of the seafood is good, with some of the ingredients imported from the UK, such as lobsters from Scotland. Dim sum is popular at lunch and, during Chinese festivals, handmade products like glutinous rice dumplings and mooncakes are provided.

这家高级粤菜厅由来自伦敦的皇朝集团开设，以供应鲍鱼、鱼肚等海味及海鲜等高级广东菜式为主。厨师注重选材用料，部分菜式用上独家从英国进口的食材，例如苏格兰龙虾和带子。午膳时间可品尝各款自制广东点心。在传统节日，更有自制应节食品如粽子等出售。

SHANGHAI
上海

TEL.+86 21 6333 2981

3F, Bund 5, 20 Guangdong Road, Huangpu

黄浦区广东路20号外滩5号3楼

www.royalchinagroup.com

Royal China Club

SHANGHAI
上海

TEL.+86 21 5877 3786

2F, Pudong Shangri-La Hotel, 33 Fu Cheng Road, Pudong

浦东新区富城路33号浦东香格里拉
大酒店2楼

www.seventhson.hk

🍴

SEVENTH SON (PUDONG)
家全七福（浦东新区）

Having seven branches spread across China, Hong Kong and Japan means that this restaurant group has plenty of experience when it comes to Cantonese food. Their philosophy here is to import top class ingredients and allow their quality to shine through. Located within a luxury hotel, the restaurant provides a comfortable setting to go with the views of the Huangpu River. The experience is further enhanced by the attentive and professional service.

家全七福在中国、香港和日本等亚洲地区共有七家食店，秉承在香港的总店致力炮制传统高级粤菜的精神，此店供应的粤菜不光选料上乘，且绝不卖弄花巧，纯以天然简单的调味料和扎实细腻的烹调功夫制作出风味正宗的菜肴。服务员贴心灵巧的服务令用餐体验生色不少。

Seventh Son

SHÀNG-XÍ
尚席

Marble floors, luxurious fabrics and impressive chandeliers add to the elegance of this Chinese restaurant which evokes the colonial style from the time of the French Concession. The menu is largely Cantonese but there are Shanghainese specialities too, as well as some personalised touches from the chef who is committed to creating healthy dishes by using less oil. Try the crispy tofu with barbecue pork, or the shrimp dumpling with truffle.

深棕色凹凸有致的墙壁、别具气派的大理石地面，配上高贵的布艺座椅和偌大的水晶吊灯，营造出法国殖民时期的典雅气息。餐单以广东菜为主，也有少量上海菜和别具特色的新创作，大厨着重味道之余也追求健康，特意减少油和糖的使用，黑松露虾饺皇和层酥红烧肉均是其招牌名菜。

SHANGHAI
上海

TEL.+86 21 2036 1310

2F, Four Seasons Pudong, 210 Century Avenue, Pudong

浦东新区世纪大道210号浦东四季酒店2楼

www.fourseasons.com/pudong/

ASIA 亚洲

Shàng-Xí

SUMMER PALACE
夏宫

There are three distinct areas to this smart and sumptuously decorated Cantonese restaurant, with each one serving its own speciality. In the Pantry you'll find dim sum; it's claypot classics in the Lantern; and the Imperial for sophisticated and classic Cantonese cooking which is overseen by a chef with many years' experience in Hong Kong. The private dining rooms are very impressive, as is the wine list.

餐馆分为三个区域：供应点心的厨房区、提供传统经典砂锅菜的灯笼厅及专侍精细高级的经典粤菜的皇家厅。有品质的高级家具摆设及雅致的装潢，室内环境高贵且有气派。高素质的食物水准，在大后方担任指挥工作、富经验的香港主厨应记一功。优秀的酒单用来接待珍贵的客人最适合不过。

SHANGHAI
上海

TEL.+86 21 2203 8888

3F, Jing An Shangri-La Hotel, 1218 Middle Yan'an Road, Jingan

静安区延安中路1218号静安香格里拉大酒店3楼

www.shangri-la.com/jingan

Summer Palace

🍴

WEI JING GE
蔚景阁

Exposed ceiling rafters add to the sense that you're eating in a hidden attic at the Waldorf Astoria. This formal restaurant is enhanced by some big pieces of reproduction art, including a large mural. The Hong Kong born chef delivers a sophisticated Cantonese menu that showcases his talents, as well as number of classic Shanghainese specialities prepared with equal care. The weekend dim sum is always popular, so be sure to book early.

蔚景阁置身于充满历史感的上海总会旧址内,装潢免不了受到其怀旧风影响:复古的横梁雕木、沈稳的中式地毯、画功细致的壁画,令你仿如身处上世纪三、四十年代的高级中菜食府。来自香港的大厨凭经验和天赋制作出多道烹调精细、风味尤佳的粤菜和数道经典沪菜。周末早午点心拼餐经常一座难求。

SHANGHAI
上海

TEL.+86 21 6322 9988
5F, Waldorf Astoria Hotel, 2 Zhongshan Dong Yi Road, Huangpu
黄浦区中山东一路2号华尔道夫酒店5楼
www.waldorfastoriashanghai.com

♿ 🛋 🅿 🕐🍴

SHANGHAI
上海

TEL.+86 21 6261 4333

3F, 396 West Yan'an Road, Jingan

静安区延安西路396号3楼

🍴○

WISCA (JINGAN)
惠食佳（静安）

The Wisca group originated in Guangzhou and now has two branches in Shanghai serving their Cantonese specialities. This one comes with a fish pool and plenty of bamboo which lend a certain serenity to proceedings. The seafood dishes are the most popular choices on the menu although the famed casseroles are also well worth ordering. There are private rooms available upstairs.

广州的惠食佳把精致创新的粤菜带到上海，共有两家分店。静安区这家店子环境雅致，大厅以鱼池和竹子营造出安逸平静的氛围，桌子与桌子之间保持着充足空间，包厢设在上层。这里最受欢迎的是海鲜菜式，鱼、虾、蟹等均有多种不同的方法烹调。驰名的一系列煲仔菜也不能错过。

WISCA (PUDONG)
惠食佳（浦东新区）

There's a lighter, whiter colour scheme to this branch from the Wisca group and the atmosphere is comfortable and relaxing. Cantonese seafood dishes are the main draw, but when the casserole dishes are finished off at the tableside and the aroma fills the room you'll regret not ordering one yourself. The restaurant is also equipped with a wood-burning grill to cook its ducks.

源自广州的惠食佳以精致创新的粤菜驰名，后发展至上海。在浦东的这家分店，素白色的环境令心神放松。包厢分布在三楼，四楼的大厅中设有燃木烤鸭炉。海鲜是这儿的主角，此外，还有多款滋味煲仔菜，当中有不少是现煮菜式，故室内总是弥漫着诱人香气。

SHANGHAI
上 海

TEL.+86 21 5820 3333

3-4F, Shanghai Merchants Tower, 161 East Lujiazui Road, Pudong

浦东新区陆家嘴东路161号招商局大厦3-4楼

Michelin

XIN YUAN LOU
馨源楼

A 1920s French colonial-style villa plays host to this Cantonese restaurant boasting plenty of old world charm thanks to its period furniture, fireplace and Chinese artwork. It's spread over two floors and includes a bar, a lounge, a tea room and several private rooms. The menu is mostly Cantonese but there are some Shanghainese dishes, with popular choices being pan-fried chicken with black truffle, and sautéed crystal shrimps with egg white.

SHANGHAI
上海

TEL.+86 21 6472 5222

InterContinental Ruijin Hotel, 118 Ruijin Er Road, Huangpu

黄浦区瑞金二路118号瑞金洲际酒店

www.intercontinental.com

餐厅坐落于瑞金洲际酒店主楼旁的一幢三层红砖西式洋楼中，划为茶室、客厅、酒吧和多个独立包厢，四周布满中式艺术品、火炉、古典风格的吊灯及家具，洋溢着浓浓的老上海风情，顶层的景观露台更可俯瞰花园美景。这儿提供粤菜和本帮菜，黑松露鸡、玻璃明虾炒蛋白、日式特酱鳕鱼等均是受欢迎菜式。

Xin Yuan Lou

ZIFU HUI
子福慧

This is haute couture in culinary terms – exquisite courses tailored to diners' liking. It specialises in river fish from Nantong, alongside up-market Cantonese fare. The freshest ingredients are skilfully prepared and MSG is banished from the kitchen. Besides the serene Zen-inspired main dining room, seven private rooms are available. As roast meats and double-boiled soups take time to make, reservations are highly recommended.

SHANGHAI
上海

TEL.+86 21 3388 7577

Building C2, Yunfeng Villa, 1665 Hongqiao Road, Changning

长宁区虹桥路1665号云峰别墅 C2幢

供应精品江鲜粤菜的子福慧定位为高档私宴订制餐厅,标榜选用最新鲜的原材料、精细的烹饪技巧和不添加味精,以还原食材原味。其中江鲜皆来自有鱼米之乡美誉的南通。餐厅装潢风格与菜式相搭配,以"静"、"思"概念设计,简约中充满禅意,并设七间厢房。由于烧味及炖汤处理需时,建议先行预订。

TAIPEI
台北

❀ ❀ ❀

LE PALAIS
颐宫

Chef Chan moved to Taiwan from Macau nearly 20 years ago and specialises in Cantonese cuisine of the highest quality. The lavishly furnished dining room feels modern and chic, but with nice traditional touches such as ceramic art, calligraphy and paintings. The cooking is truly outstanding, with the Cantonese-style crispy roast duck, the tofu dishes and the baked egg custard tarts especially impressive; consider pre-ordering the roast baby duck. Service is thoughtful and friendly.

各式各样的瓷器和仿古书画令环境于传统中不失格调。细看餐垫，印上了本年度的天干地支、对应时令的食材墨宝和诗词，足见餐厅的用心和细致。自2000年由澳门来台发展的陈师傅一直专注广东菜式，且坚持事事亲力亲为，需预订的先知鸭和火焰片皮鸭是其巧手之作，豆腐菜式更展现其出神入化的功架，点菜时不妨预留一份原味蛋塔。

TAIPEI
台北

TEL.+886 2 2181 9985

17F, Palais de Chine Hotel, 3, Section 1, Chengde Road, Datong
大同区承德路一段3号君品酒店
17楼

www.palaisdechinehotel.com

 ♿ 🍴 📶 🅿

TAIPEI
台北

TEL.+886 2 2381 7180
46 Hengyang Road, Zhongzheng
中正区衡阳路46号
www.3coins.com.tw

THREE COINS
大三元

It's owned by an artist, frequented by socialites and generously adorned with antiques and art pieces. At night, the opulent glass building, with oversized Chinese calligraphy on its walls, even glows in different colours. The menu is classic Cantonese, with occasional Taiwanese touches. Regulars come for their Peking duck served with wholemeal flatbread; steamed abalone with fresh and sundried tomatoes; and chicken soup with bitter tea seed oil.

楼高六层、饶有气势的书法外墙,会否增加了在此用餐的兴味?店内装潢古雅,各式古董、书法、字画、艺术品放满四周,艺文气氛浓厚,难怪成为政商名人会面倾谈的热门场所。这儿提供的广东菜带点台式元素,例如鲜茄大鲜鲍,是蒸鲍鱼配以干鲜番茄和九层塔进食,清新可喜;苦茶油鸡汤也蛮受欢迎。

Three Coins

YA GE
雅阁

A narrow corridor with Asian antiques leads to this square-shaped and classically-styled Cantonese restaurant on the 3rd floor of the Mandarin Oriental. Semi-private booths on the sides and at the back are the ones to go for. The vast choice includes various set menus (such as hairy crab when in season) and an array of Cantonese classics, some with a personal twist added by the experienced chef. Service is efficient and formal.

步进隐闭的入口,放眼狭长的走廊两旁尽是中式古董摆设。方正的餐室以华丽的布艺和木屏风装饰,格调典雅,大型吊灯成为全场焦点。两侧的半独立厢座或后方的U型餐桌是较佳的用餐位置。厚甸甸的餐牌上罗列的传统粤菜不失主厨个人风格,其丰富经验可见一斑。秋季时分更设大闸蟹菜式。

TAIPEI
台北

TEL.+886 2 2715 6788

3F, Mandarin Oriental Hotel, 158 Dunhua North Road, Songshan

松山区敦化北路158号
文华东方酒店3楼

www.mandarinoriental.com/taipei

PENG FAMILY
彭家园

The owner-chef moved to Taiwan from Hong Kong over 35 years ago to bring authentic Cantonese cooking to the island. The décor of his family-run restaurant may be rather old-school but the crystal ceiling lamps, red carpet and Chinese paintings are welcoming and familiar. Seafood dishes, such as silky egg white custard with scallops, fried crab with glass noodles in clay pot, and steamed seafood, are prized for their precise cooking.

TAIPEI
台北

TEL.+886 2 2704 5152
60 Dongfeng Street, Da'an
大安区东丰街60号

⇆ ⓞ⌁ ⑤

规模不大的餐厅属家族生意，红地毯、水晶吊灯加上中式挂画，是典型粤菜餐馆格局，服务多年的店员令店子充溢亲切感。来自香港的大厨兼店东扎根台湾三十多年，致力为本地食客带来不卖弄花巧的传统广东味道。他对烹调的时间拿捏准确，尤其擅长清蒸海鲜菜式，此外，芋泥酥鸭、琼山豆腐和螃蟹粉丝煲也是推介之选。

Michelin

GAC MOTOR | THE ROAD TO GREATNESS

Have Courage
Be fearless,
the brave are the pioneers of greatness.

From Ordinary to Extraordinary.
Make the Leap

勇　担　当

无惧重负
勇敢者面前才有路

平凡到伟大

一

步

ZUI FENG YUAN
醉枫园小馆

At this sister restaurant to Peng Family, the chef insists on cooking Cantonese food exactly the way his great uncle did. Lamb belly hot pot is a winter speciality made with Australian lamb, red bean curd, sugarcane and ginger. Equally popular is crispy duck stuffed with mashed taro, steamed egg white custard with scallops and fish head hot pot. Service is friendly and warm and reservations are recommended on holidays.

掌厨的彭师傅一直遵从叔公配方烹调，虽然与彭家园的厨师师承同一人，大家的手法还是大相径庭。他烹调的是粤菜，芋泥香酥鸭、琼山豆腐尤其出色。冬季记得一试羊腩火锅或鱼头火锅，前者以澳洲草羊、甘蔗头、老姜和南乳炮制；后者强调原汁原味，与坊间用沙茶酱的做法有别。服务员训练有素，并记住客人喜好。假期前后特别繁忙，建议订座。

TAIPEI
台北

TEL.+886 2 2577 9528

5, Lane 8, Section 3, Bade Road, Songshan

松山区八德路三段8巷5号

Michelin

CANTON COURT

粤菜厅

This simple dining room blends a modern décor with traditional Chinese tones, while teapots on the walls add fun touches to that theme. Just like its name, the food shows solid accomplished skills without being over-embellished. Regulars come for the chicken soup with dried fish maw and steamed lobster with Shaoxing wine and chicken oil. Exquisite Cantonese dim sum made in-house is served all day.

TAIPEI
台北

TEL.+886 2 2100 2100

2F, Ambassador Hotel, 63, Section 2, Zhongshan North Road, Zhongshan

中山区中山北路二段63号2楼

www.ambassador-hotels.com

整齐有致的茶壶一列列挂在墙上,既有趣又不失中国味道,简单中见心思。顾名思义,餐厅以粤菜为主,菜式一如其名扎实不花巧,餐单上罗列多款巧手菜式,包括招牌菜花胶浓汤煲土鸡和鸡油花雕蒸龙虾。点心亦是叫好之作,由经验丰富的点心厨师主理,除了早午时段应市,连晚市亦有供应。

Canton Court

MY HUMBLE HOUSE
寒舍食谱

Despite its name, the dining room itself is not too humble – the red carpet, black furniture and the oversized ink painting on the wall speak loudly of style and luxury. The menu is authentically Cantonese, but the quality ingredients are unmistakably Taiwanese. The spice marinated baby roast duck uses cherry ducks from Yilan County, with juicy tender meat and crisp skin. Cantonese dim sum turnip cake is fried and spiced up with XO sauce.

低调谦卑的名字，配以红黑色主调的装潢、给人深刻印象的水墨画作，足见这是一家品味卓绝、处处皆经慎思密想的餐馆。主厨虽然祖籍台湾，但烹调粤菜经验到家，优质材料，辅以精湛烹调技巧，所呈献的传统菜式没有叫人失望，脆皮先知鸭和XO酱干炒萝卜糕只是其得意之作中的少数。

TAIPEI
台北

TEL.+886 2 6622 8018

2F, Le Méridien Hotel, 38 Songren Road, Xinyi

信义区松仁路38号寒舍艾美酒店2楼

www.lemeridien.com/taipei

ASIA 亚洲

SHANG PALACE
香宫

The beautiful reception sets the scene for the Cantonese meal that will unfold. The elegant corridor and tea station continue the stylish look while bespoke charger plates, napkin rings and chopstick rests cast in gold-coloured glass complement the ambiance perfectly. Led by a head chef from Hong Kong, the kitchen team prepares authentic and classic Cantonese dishes with skill.

电梯引领食客来到酒店六楼，精心布置的接待处让人印象深刻，典雅的走廊和品茶专区设计同样贯彻水准，餐桌上，餐巾和筷箸置于精美的玻璃食器之上，从装潢至装饰皆叫人翘首以待。食物同样没有令人失望，由香港主厨领军的厨师团队带来一系列传统经典广东菜肴，每道菜都尽显功架和娴熟的烹调技巧。

TAIPEI
台北

TEL.+886 2 2378 6886

6F, Shangri-La's Far Eastern Plaza Hotel, 201, Section 2, Dunhua South Road, Da'an

大安区敦化南路二段201号
香格里拉远东国际大饭店6楼

www.shangri-la.com/taipei

ASIA 亚洲

STEVENLIN /Shang Palace

SILKS HOUSE
晶华轩

The corridor that leads to the dining room is adorned with Chinese calligraphy of a famous poem etched on glass screens and backlit on the perforated wall; there's even an impressive water feature at one end. Cantonese classics make up the main part of the menu, alongside a few Sichuan options for those who fancy more heat in their food. For a romantic dinner, request a table behind the partition screens.

长长的书法走廊引领你到达这家粤菜餐厅，沿路走来，铁划银钩的草书字体刻满玻璃造景，灯光投射之下那家喻户晓的诗词跃然而出，走廊尽处的流水装饰叫人屏息，未安座视觉已获得大大满足。餐单上尽是经典的粤式菜肴，厨师同时加入少量四川菜式，满足嗜辣的饕客。欲享私人空间不妨预订包厢。

TAIPEI
台北

TEL.+886 2 2522 8236

3F, Regent Hotel, 3, Lane 39, Section 2, Zhongshan North Road, Zhongshan

中山区中山北路二段39巷3号晶华酒店3楼

www.regenttaipei.com

James Chen/Silks House

THE DRAGON
辰园

Pre-booking is recommended at this spacious restaurant boasting a contemporary décor, with Chinese details, tan wood finishes and comfy chairs adding to the feeling of serenity. The kitchen is run by experienced chefs specialising in Cantonese cuisine. Signature dishes include stir-fried pork tendons in XO sauce, crispy barbecued pork, roast baby duck (pre-order needed) and Cantonese-style Peking duck (in strictly limited quantities).

选址地库无减餐厅的吸引力，深棕色木屏风配以同色系的墙身，拼合出带中国色彩的餐室，传统中不失时尚，宽敞的环境加上舒适的靠背椅更适合宴客和商务聚餐。菜式由多位擅长广东菜的厨师主理，叫好之作众多，包括须预订的脆皮先知鸭、限量供应的广式片皮鸭、脆皮叉烧和XO酱炒龙筋，难怪总是坐无虚席。

TAIPEI
台北

TEL.+886 2 2321 1818

B1, Sheraton Grand Hotel, 12, Section 1, Zhongxiao East Road, Zhongzheng
中正区忠孝东路一段12号喜来登大饭店B1

www.sheratongrandtaipei.com

The Dragon

TOH-KA-LIN
桃花林

An outpost of the 50-year-old Tokyo restaurant with the same name, it sports a classic Chinese décor with opulent contemporary touches. The elaborate menu shows a strong Cantonese influence and specialises in luxury seafood, such as abalone and sea cucumber. Live lobster and grouper from the tank are popular among diners, but the barbecue meat and claypot dishes are also worth checking out. Sit at the cosy sofa booths for more privacy.

来自东京的桃花林本店经营超过半世纪，这店子一脉相承，传统的中式装潢带有现代元素，以红色作主调的中式桌椅并以玻璃屏风，满墙的瓷器摆设是焦点所在。餐单偏于粤菜风味，尤以海鲜如鲍鱼和海参等为强项，烧味或砂锅小菜亦不容忽视。沙发卡座私密度高，适合商务午餐。

TAIPEI
台北

TEL.+886 2 2181 5136

3F, Okura Prestige Hotel, 9, Section 1, Nanjing East Road, Zhongshan
中山区南京东路一段9号大仓久和大饭店3楼

www.okurataipei.com.tw

ASIA 亚洲

SEOUL
首尔

✿

JIN JIN

For over 40 years, Chef Wang Yuk Sung has been committed to popularizing Chinese cuisine in Korea. Unlike most generic Korean-style Chinese restaurants ubiquitous to Seoul, Chef Wang offers a limited menu of just 10 dishes at his restaurant to ensure that the quality of the food he serves is consistently high. Some of the most requested dishes include shrimp toast, stir-fried king crab, mapo tofu and stir-fried beef with gai lan. There are three locations of Jin Jin in Seoul. The original location in Seogyo-dong is only open for dinner.

四十多年来，主厨一直致力在韩国推广中式料理。与首尔的大多数韩式中餐馆不同，这餐厅只提供有限度的十道菜式，以确保维持食物的高素质。最受欢迎的美食包括虾多士、炒大螃蟹、麻婆豆腐和芥兰炒牛肉等。首尔有三家分店，西桥洞这家原店只开晚市。

SEOUL
首尔

TEL.+82 70-5035-8878
123 jandori-ro, Mapo-gu

☏🍴

SEOUL
首尔

TEL.+82 2-6388-5500

11F Four Seasons Hotel, 97
Saemunan-ro

www.fourseasons.com/seoul

YU YUAN

Inspired by the glitz and glamour of 1920's Shanghai, interior designer André Fu's dining room is drop-dead gorgeous with its alluring jade-colored walls, marbled floors, lavish furniture and refined tableware. The menu features mostly Cantonese dishes, but also offers recipes from other Chinese regions. Highlights include Pecking Duck, crispy pork belly and Cantonese-style steamed sea bream. Their weekend dim sum brunch is extremely popular.

室内设计师傅厚民（André Fu）的餐厅以1920年代上海的浮奢气派为主调，令人惊艳的碧玉色墙壁、大理石地板、豪华的家具和精致的餐具搭配得华丽夺目。餐厅的菜肴以粤式为主，辅以中国其他地区的菜式，驰名之作包括北京烤鸭、脆皮烧腩肉和粤式清蒸鲷鱼。此外，餐厅每逢周末推出的点心早午拼餐极受欢迎。

Yu Yuan

SANDONG GYOJAKWAN

Sandong Gyojakwan is helmed by Chinese-Korean Chef Dan Byeong-ho who learned the art of dumpling making from his parents at the tender young age of ten. His Apgujeong restaurant specializes in Chinese-style dumplings, prepared from scratch, daily, from the wrappers to the filling. Boiled dumplings and steamed dumplings each offer a different texture, due to the difference in the thickness of the skin. Other items on the menu include Korean-Chinese staples like five-spice beef salad, XO shrimp and stir-fried assorted delicacies. Seating is limited to four tables.

餐厅由有中韩血统的主厨主理，他在十岁之龄便从父母身上习得了做饺子的技巧。这家位处狎鸥亭的店子专门供应自制的中式饺子，从饺子皮至馅料均每天现做。水煮和蒸饺的皮厚薄不一，是以有不同的口感。菜单上也有其他中韩经典菜式，诸如五香牛肉色拉、XO酱炒虾球和各式小炒等。店子座位有限，只有四张桌子。

SEOUL
首尔

TEL.+82 2-514-2608
214 Apgujeong-ro, Gangnam-gu

Weilou

BAEK NI HYANG

Cantonese-style cuisine prevails at this high-end Chinese restaurant, but it also features a good range of Beijing-style and Sichuan-style cuisine. Executive Chef Wang Chuan Sheng is a respected veteran, who offers a wide array of classic Chinese dishes, including delicacies like Buddha Jumps over the Wall and the more recognizable sweet and sour pork with honey. Perched on the 57th floor of Yeouido's iconic 63 Building, the restaurant offers stunning vistas of the city.

这家高级中餐厅以粤菜闻名，京式和川式菜肴亦不遑多让。行政总厨Wang Chuan Sheng是一位备受敬重的老行家，精于烹调各种经典中国菜肴，包括佛跳墙和具代表性的糖醋猪肉。餐厅位于汝矣岛（Yeouido）地标63大厦的第57层，可以俯瞰壮丽的城市景观。

SEOUL
首尔

TEL.+82 2-789-5741
57F, 63 Building, 50 63-ro, Yeongdeungpo-gu
www.63restaurant.co.kr

ASIA 亚洲

Baek Ni Hyang

CRYSTAL JADE

Crystal Jade first opened its doors in Singapore in 1991 as a Cantonese restaurant. More than two decades later, the restaurant chain operates in many countries across Asia, including Korea with 11 locations just in Seoul. Crystal Jade's mission is to serve high-quality regional cuisine from China. Classics like Hong Kong-style dim sum, sautéed prawns and scallops in XO sauce and sautéed chicken in black bean sauce are perennial favorites.

翡翠最初是一家粤菜餐馆，于1991年在新加坡开业。二十多年后，这家餐饮连锁店在亚洲多个国家都开展了业务，单在首尔就有十一家分店。集团的使命是提供高品质的中国地方菜式，经典菜肴有如港式点心、XO酱爆虾球带子及豆豉炒鸡球等，都是历久不衰的受欢迎菜式。

SEOUL
首尔

TEL.+82 2-3789-8088

B1F, 16 Namdaemun-ro 7-gil, Jung-gu

www.crystaljade.co.kr

Crystal Jade

HONG BO GAK

For a taste of authentic Cantonese and Sichuan cuisine, head over to Hong Bo Gak on the 2nd floor of Grand Ambassador Pullman. The restaurant - helmed by a veteran chef dedicated to popularizing Chinese cuisine in Korea - offers a full-course Chinese-style dining experience as well as à la carte and seasonal menus. Stand-out dishes include Buddha Jumps Soup, fried king prawn stuffed with mixed seafood mousse and garlic sauce, and stir-fried minced beef balls.

如果想品尝正宗的粤菜和川菜，可前往大使铂尔曼酒店二楼的红宝阁。餐厅由一位致力在韩国推广中国菜、经验丰富的厨师掌舵，除了提供中式套餐的餐饮体验，还有单点菜肴和时令推介。招牌菜包括佛跳墙及海鲜慕斯酿皇帝虾配蒜蓉酱等。

ASIA 亚洲

SEOUL
首尔

TEL.+82 2-2270-3141

2F Grand Ambassador Pullman, 287 Dongho-ro, Jung-gu

www.grand.ambatel.com/seoul

Hong Bo Gak

HONG YUAN

Instantly memorable with its crimson décor, this high-end restaurant at The Westin Chosun Seoul, specializes in Cantonese cuisine. The elegant space offers a taste of the best in Chinese-style formal dining, with its classic yet innovate dishes. Hong Yuan's commitment to using the freshest ingredients to make healthy and tasty food is unparalleled, as seen in its heavy use of ingredients like seafood, Tofu and vegetables. Live music during dinner service.

这家专门供应粤菜的高级餐厅位于首尔威斯汀朝鲜酒店,深红色的装潢令人瞬间一见难忘,陈设空间品味优雅,菜式经典而不乏创意,是顶级中式正规餐饮的氛围。红缘使用最新鲜食材制作健康美食的承诺乃无可比拟,一如所言的运用了大量海鲜、豆腐和蔬菜。晚餐时段有现场音乐演奏。

SEOUL
首尔

TEL.+82 2-317-0494
1F Westin Chosun Hotel, 106 Sogong-ro, Jung-gu
www.echosunhotel.com

ASIA
亚洲

Hong Yuan

TOH LIM

Located on the 37th floor of Lotte Hotel, Toh Lim offers a state-of-the-art Chinese fine dining experience. The restaurant is acclaimed for its expert handling of ingredients, whose natural flavors shine through in the individual dishes. Led by Chef Yeo Kyung-ok, a highly-respected veteran of Korea's culinary industry, the team serves up a wide array of Chinese dishes, with a special focus on Cantonese-style cuisine. Private rooms are available.

桃林位于乐天酒店37楼，为食客带来别开生面的中式美食体验。餐厅处理食材的专业手法赢得一致赞誉，保留天然的味道令每一道菜生色不少。餐厅团队由备受尊崇的韩国厨师吕敬玉（Yeo Kyung-ok）领导，提供各式各样的中国美食，其中以粤菜为主打菜肴。餐厅设有私人厢房。

SEOUL
首尔

TEL.+82 2-317-7101
37F Lotte Hotel, 30 Eulji-ro, Jung-gu
www.lottehotel.com/seoul

ASIA 亚洲

Toh Lim

ASIA 亚洲

233

OSAKA
大阪

KOKYU

This very comfortable restaurant is ideal for anniversaries and celebrations; it is named after the Forbidden City and features Cantonese cuisine. We recommend the 'Steamed Awabi with Chinese Dried Food Soup' – dried scallop, ginseng, and other ingredients are added, and steamed for six hours, adding a savouriness to the soup. The mango pudding is made like a soup with tapioca and grapefruit.

这家餐厅非常舒适，很适合在此庆祝纪念日和节日。它以北京故宫命名，菜单以粤菜为主。推荐佛跳墙，加入了瑶柱、人参和其他食材一起炖制六小时，为汤增添了一份鲜味。芒果布丁是以加入西米和葡萄柚的杨枝甘露制成。

OSAKA
大阪

TEL.+816 6440 1065

3F, Westin, 1-1-20 Oyodonaka, Kita-ku, Osaka, 531-0076

www.westin-osaka.co.jp

TOKYO
东京

SENSE

Ambient lighting and panoramic views make dinner here all the more enjoyable – just be sure to ask for a window table. The chef is thoroughly versed in Cantonese cuisine and his credo is to faithfully reproduce traditional cuisine. Specialities include deep-fried whole pigeon, yakuzen soup with ginseng, and quickly-steamed star grouper. We also recommend the dim sum.

餐厅的灯光布置和全景景观令用膳过程更添惬意,但请要求安排靠窗的桌子。厨师精通粤菜,他的信念是忠实地将传统美食重现。特色菜包括石岐脆皮烧乳鸽、人参药膳汤和蒸东星斑。点心也是值得推荐的。

TOKYO
东京

TEL.+813-3270-8188

37F, Mandarin Oriental, 2-1-1 Nihombashi-muromachi, Chuo-ku, Tokyo, 103-8328

www.mandarinoriental.co.jp/tokyo

SINGAPORE
新加坡

CHEF KANG'S
江师傅

Chef Kang brings his experience of over 40 years to bear at this simply furnished eatery. The room is more about practicality than luxury – and likewise his cooking largely eschews expensive ingredients to focus instead on creating traditional and satisfying Cantonese dishes. His many loyal customers vouch for his ability – follow their lead and go on a culinary trip by opting for his 'omakase' menu.

毫不沾染世俗尘烟的小店、门牌亦简单地以"江师傅"作招徕。顾名思义，江师就是这儿的主厨，他对烹饪有一份坚持，从不假手于人，更会亲自到市场采购食材，甚至不惜功本购入各种野生鱼类，让客人品尝到有素质且味美的菜肴。订座时切记询问哪些时令菜式需要预订，五人或以上建议尝尝厨师发办。

SINGAPORE
新加坡

TEL.+65 6238 6263
25 Mackenzie Road, Little India
麦肯西路25号

ASIA
亚洲

CRYSTAL JADE GOLDEN PALACE
翡翠金阁

SINGAPORE
新加坡

TEL.+65 6734 6866

**Paragon Shopping Centre, #05-22,
290 Orchard Road, Orchard**

乌节路290号百利宫#05-22

www.crystaljade.com

Opened in 2002, this is the most comfortable branch of this restaurant group and the only one which specialises in Chao Zhou dishes, like cold crab and sugar-coated yam. Look out too for the Cantonese barbecue meat and assorted seafood dishes; more contemporary offerings include chilled foie gras with sake and roasted suckling pig with black truffle. Their wine cellar includes a good international selection.

集团内唯一一间有潮州菜供应的食府，餐单上大部分均是传统潮州菜如冻蟹、反沙芋等，还有粤式烧味、海鲜菜式和午市的即制点心。此外，还有一些较新派的菜式如清酒鹅肝、黑松露乳猪饭卷等，不妨一试。

Crystal Jade Golden Palace

IMPERIAL TREASURE FINE
TEOCHEW CUISINE (ORCHARD)
御宝阁（乌节）

It may have moved to new premises in a large shopping mall at the end of 2016, but this pleasantly dressed Chao Zhou restaurant is bright and relaxing, thanks to its large windows. It offers various traditional Chao Zhou dishes, including some which are not so easy to find these days, like pan-fried taro with prawns or steamed cold mud crabs. With some dishes, you have the option of ordering a smaller portion.

于2016年迁至区内更大型的商场内，室内设计焕然一新，大片玻璃窗引入自然光，气氛轻松。餐厅供应的传统潮州菜选择丰富，个别菜式如惹味香脆的鲜虾芋头烙及每日限量供应的鲜滑冻黄膏蟹，并不常见。此外，大部分菜式都有大、小份量供应，让食客点菜时更有弹性。

SINGAPORE
新加坡

TEL.+65 6736 2118

ION Orchard, #03-05, 2 Orchard Turn, Orchard
乌节弯路2号乌节Ion大厦#03-05
www.imperialtreasure.com

ASIA 亚洲

Imperial Treasure Fine Teochew Cuisine

JIANG-NAN CHUN
江南春

The exquisite space, reached via a marble staircase, is warm and welcoming and its heavy leather chairs are especially comfortable. In 2017 Chef Lam, with over 20 years' experience in Cantonese cooking, joined the kitchen. Apart from traditional dishes, his signatures like deep-fried chicken with fresh lemon sauce and wok-fried star grouper fillet with superior soy sauce are obvious highlights. Reservations recommended.

SINGAPORE
新加坡

TEL.+65 6831 7250

Four Seasons Hotel, Level 2, 190 Orchard Boulevard, Orchard
乌节林荫道190号四季酒店2层
www.fourseasons.com/singapore

从四季酒店第一层的大理石楷梯拾级而上即可到达。餐厅富亚洲风情,装饰雅致温暖,厚厚的皮革座椅予人舒适之感。餐单以粤菜肴为主,主理广东菜逾二十年的林师傅于2017年加盟后,除了保留传统广东菜外,更加添了其首本名菜,包括鲜柠汁脆皮炸子鸡及头抽干煎东星件。餐厅不论何时皆座无虚席,建议订座。

ASIA 亚洲

Jiang-Nan Chun

LEI GARDEN
利苑

Unlike the other restaurants in the group, this one comes with a more European feel to its decoration, in keeping with the colonial style of the building which hosts it. What isn't different from the other branches is the menu content – so expect authentic Cantonese dishes prepared with care and good quality dim sum at lunch. It's certainly worth ordering the roasted meats and the double-boiled soups in advance.

此店的室内设计有别于集团一贯的中国风,为了与所在的殖民地建筑物互相融合,布置装潢均充满欧陆气息。然而,餐单上的菜式却与集团其他分店没什分别,食物的味道是一贯的正宗,建议预订粤式烧味和炖汤。午市点心同样吸引。

SINGAPORE
新加坡

TEL.+65 6339 3822
Chijmes, #01-24, 30 Victoria Street, City Hall
维多利亚街30号赞美广场#01-24
www.leigarden.com.cn

Lei Garden

SUMMER PALACE
夏宫

The Regent hotel's flagship restaurant is this authentic Cantonese restaurant which exudes a sense of calm and serenity. The signature dishes of the experienced head chef and his well-drilled kitchen include Five Spice deep-fried frog's legs; crispy roast pork; braised minced crabmeat in spinach soup; and fried chicken with almond flakes. The personable and professional service adds to the overall experience.

这中菜厅的装潢带浓浓中国色彩，金黄、大红等色调尽显富丽堂皇，宽敞的布置予食客宁静而舒适的用膳空间。这里由中国厨师主理，用料新鲜上乘，供应味道丰饶多姿的粤菜，招牌菜有酥炸田鸡腿、金牌脆皮烧肉、蟹肉菠菜羹及西柠杏香鸡等 。

SINGAPORE
新加坡

TEL.+65 6725 3288

Regent Hotel, Level 3, 1 Cuscaden Road, Orchard

卡斯加登路1号丽晶酒店3层

www.regenthotels.com

♿ ✥ 🍴 🅿 ☎🍴

Summer Palace

SUMMER PAVILION
夏苑

The Chihuly lounge is a great place for a drink before you're ushered into the large, contemporary dining room surrounded by a garden. You'll be well looked after as the engaging staff provide service with plenty of vim and vigour. The extensive Cantonese menu covers all bases, with seafood a particular highlight; the double-boiled sea whelk soup with fish maw, poached rice with lobster and braised abalone are just some of the specialities.

偌大的餐室被现代中式庭园包围，延伸至天花的落地玻璃窗，触目所及均景色如画，特大的餐桌赋予客人更多空间，窗边位置尤佳，欲坐得亲密点，可选择半私人卡座。细致的绘瓷用具和充满活力的服务，特显豪华气派。菜单含括最典型的粤菜，招牌菜有椰皇花胶响螺炖鸡汤、龙虾西施泡饭和蚝皇四头南非鲍鱼。

SINGAPORE
新加坡

TEL.+65 6434 5286

**The Ritz-Carlton, Millenia, Level 3,
7 Raffles Avenue, Marina Square**
莱佛士道7号丽思卡尔顿美年酒店
3层
www.ritzcarlton.com

ASIA 亚洲

Summer Pavilion

LIAO FAN HAWKER CHAN
了凡香港油鸡饭·面

What started at a stall in Chinatown Food Centre lead inevitably to Chef Chan going into partnership and opening a restaurant. Equally inevitable is the size of the queue – it forms well before opening time, such is the reputation of his delicious soy sauce chicken rice and roast pork. The new premises may provide more space and seating but, just like back at the hawker centre, you'll be sharing your table with others.

SINGAPORE
新加坡

78 Smith Street, Chinatown
史密斯街78号

还没到营业时间，已见长长的人龙在门外等候，为的只是一尝简单而味美的油鸡和烧味。主厨兼店东之一的陈先生继其在熟食小贩中心的小店后，开设了这家同样以油鸡和烧味作卖点的餐馆，这儿有空调系统且座位更多，虽仍要拼桌，但食客只为了食物的素质而来，因此一点也不在意。

ASIA 亚洲

Michelin

🍴

CAPITAL
首都

When you can claim to have been the first restaurant in Singapore to have served hairy crabs then it's little wonder you have plenty of customers and lots of regulars. The third generation of the Cheong family run the show these days, with Dad cooking, Mum serving and assorted relatives assisting. Classic Cantonese cooking is what they offer, but if it's the season go for the great value hairy crab menu – or just pop in and grab some to take home.

SINGAPORE
新加坡

TEL.+65 6222 3938
323 New Bridge Road, Tanjong Pagar
新桥路323号

这家历史悠久的粤菜酒家，主要供应经典粤菜及烧味如鹅味烧鸭，已传至第三代。掌厨的是东主的父亲，其母则带领一众亲戚在店面服务客人。每到大闸蟹季节，这家号称狮城首家供应大闸蟹的酒家皆挤满了食客，为的是享用大闸蟹套餐。食客亦可将蟹买回家按自己喜欢的方式烹调。

Michelin

CHAR

叉

Cantonese roast meats prepared in a traditional way (with just a hint of Western style) lure plenty of customers to this relaxed and friendly restaurant. There's roast duck and crispy pork belly but it's the meltingly tender BBQ pork that really stands out; other Cantonese dishes on offer include seafood and stir-fried noodles. It occupies two floors – the ground floor's large round tables make it better suited to family gatherings.

设计简约随意并富现代感,地面层设有大圆桌适合家庭用餐,楼上一层有小酒吧和方桌,适合年轻人聚会。主打广式烧味,传统做法混合西式烹调法或调味料。一定要试叉烧,外观和味道都有浓浓的怀旧气息,色深带多肥脂,入口即溶却不油腻。餐厅还供应广式小菜、海鲜和粉面。午市套餐精简而价钱合理。

ASIA 亚洲

SINGAPORE
新加坡

TEL.+65 6842 7759

363 Jalan Besar, Farrer Park

惹兰勿刹363号

www.char.com.sg

justin ong/Char

CHERRY GARDEN
樱桃园

Grace, style and opulence are the hallmarks of this revered Cantonese restaurant within the Mandarin Oriental. A wall of windows lets natural light flood the room at lunch, while at night the well-spaced tables ensure plenty of privacy for intimate dinners. The dishes, from velvety congee to delicious dumplings, are prepared with considerable care. A well-priced weekend dim sum menu offers a great way of experiencing the kitchen's ability.

粗糙的石砖墙、高悬着的红灯笼,中式古典木门后,是布置富丽堂皇、古意盎然的中菜馆。一道通往花园的玻璃门、一列偌大的玻璃窗,直接透射进内的自然光令房间充满生气。皮薄如透明、内馅汁丰味浓的意式西葫芦水晶饺滋味无穷,黑椒鳕鱼金网卷令人回味。周末和公众假期设有两组点心早午餐时段。

SINGAPORE
新加坡

TEL.+65 6885 3500
Mandarin Oriental Hotel, Level 5,
5 Raffles Avenue, Marina Square
莱佛士道5号滨海广场
文华东方酒店5层
www.mandarinoriental.com/singapore

ASIA 亚洲

Cherry Garden

EMPRESS
皇后

The designers of this chic and contemporary Cantonese restaurant, courtesy of The Privé Group, have made the most of its great location within the Asian Civilisations Museum and facing the Singapore River. As such, it's one of those rare places that works just as well for a business lunch as it does for a gathering of friends or a romantic dinner. The menu is a mix of traditional and more modern dishes, with roast meats a speciality.

SINGAPORE
新加坡

TEL.+65 6776 0777
**Asian Civilisations Museum #01-03,
1 Empress Place, City Hall**
皇后坊1号亚洲文明博物馆#01-03
www.empress.com.sg

坐落于亚洲文明博物馆内,古建筑遗风搭配时尚雅致的装潢,典雅中别具韵味。敞开着的玻璃窗门,让阳光遍洒至每个角落,清新的空气弥漫一室,同时将室内和户外区串连起来,不论置身户外还是室内也能尽览新加坡河的壮丽景色。厨师选用世界各地的食材重新演绎的粤菜带点现代风味。附设的酒吧适合各种聚会。

FENG SHUI INN

风水廷

It may be hidden away on the ground floor of Crockfords Tower but this Cantonese restaurant is well worth seeking out. The large dining room is elegantly decorated with superb lacquered panels and granite walls. The signature dishes include highly nutritious double-boiled soups, Canadian geoduck clams, crispy fish skin, and pan-fried tiger prawns. At lunch, don't miss the baked yam pastry or the steamed prawn dumplings on the list of dim sum.

由在香港从事厨师多年的经验老师傅掌厨，以极新鲜食材炮制的粤菜味道令人垂涎。青柠黄金脆鱼皮、豉油皇干煎老虎虾、古法牛柳粒等均为其拿手菜。说到粤菜，当然少不了老火汤，天天新款的风水廷老火汤是必试之选。午市点心的风水廷鲜虾饺和香芋黄金角同样不能错过。

SINGAPORE
新加坡

TEL.+65 6577 6599

Crockfords Tower, G2, Resorts World Sentosa, 8 Sentosa Gateway, Sentosa
圣淘沙桥门8号圣淘沙名胜世界康乐福豪华酒店G2
www.rwsentosa.com/dining

Feng Shui Inn

![fork and knife icon]

GEYLANG CLAYPOT RICE
芽笼瓦煲饭

The house speciality and the location are both there in the name. This modestly decorated place with its round tables and plastic chairs is all about rice cooked in a claypot over charcoal – accompanied by sausage, salted fish, chicken or cured meat. Other Cantonese dishes are also on offer, such as their delicious bean curd 'prawn ball'. As the rice takes 30mins to cook, call ahead to book a table and pre-order your rice to shorten the waiting time.

餐厅位于芽笼保留区，两旁全是两层高的殖民地时期建筑，临街一面保留着昔日面貌。招牌菜是以炭火炮制的粤式瓦锅煲仔饭，腊肠、润肠、咸鱼、鸡、腊肉等材料集于一锅。此外还供应广式小菜、蒸海鲜，以自制豆腐煮成的豆腐虾球也不错。需致电预约，店方会因应人数和到达时间准备好煲仔饭。

SINGAPORE
新加坡

TEL.+65 6744 4574

639 Lorong 33, Geylang
芽笼33巷639号

![icons]

GOLDEN PEONY
金牡丹

There's a sophisticated and elegant feel to this spacious and comfortable Chinese restaurant on the 3rd floor of the Conrad Centennial hotel. Like the decoration, the Cantonese cuisine adds contemporary touches to a classic base. The best known signature dishes of the longstanding chef include double-boiled baby abalone soup with conpoy and bamboo, and braised Dong Po pork belly with crispy bun. Dim sum is also popular here.

位于康莱德酒店内，时尚与古典融合为一的布置、宽敞且高雅的环境，与由经验厨师预备的粤菜配合得天衣无缝。鲜螺头炖竹笙柱脯鲍鱼仔汤及东坡肉伴炸馒头是招牌菜。点心种类不少且素质不错。

SINGAPORE
新加坡

TEL.+65 6432 7482

Conrad Centennial Hotel, Level 3, 2 Temasek Boulevard, Marina Square
淡马锡林荫道2号康莱德酒店3层
www.conradsingapore.com

ASIA 亚洲

🍴

HUA TING
华厅

The cooking at Orchard Hotel's Cantonese restaurant comes with a contemporary flourish, with signature dishes like sautéed prawns with avocado and salted egg yolk; stewed oxtail with garlic in brown sauce; and crispy roast duck. If you've come for dim sum do try the steamed bean curd with assorted vegetables. The room is comfortable and classically decorated and is run with considerable professionalism by a team willing to offer advice.

TEL.+65 6739 6666
Orchard Hotel, Level 2, 442 Orchard Road, Orchard
乌节路442号乌节大酒店2层
www.huatingsingapore.sg

♿ ♻ 🍴 🅿 ⏰🍽

要进入这家位处酒店内的高级粤菜厅,千万别穿短裤或拖鞋,餐厅经理会对衣冠不整的人拒诸门外。餐厅装潢典雅,职员态度友善,来自香港的主厨锺立辉师傅为广东菜添上不少创意,这里的点心尤其出色,特别推荐双色两味鸳鸯虾球、蒜子红炆牛尾、脆皮烧鸭及点心腐皮上素包。

Hua Ting

IMPERIAL TREASURE CANTONESE CUISINE (GREAT WORLD CITY)
御宝轩（世界城）

The fish tanks and wine cellar at the entrance set the tone for this well-dressed Cantonese restaurant, with its wood panelling and splashes of red. It offers a comprehensive selection of Cantonese dishes, with set menus for 2 to 10 people. Look out for the braised fish maw with goose web. Dim sum, prepared by the restaurant's Hong Kong chefs, is available daily. It is part of the Imperial Treasure Group, which has over 20 restaurants.

隶属御宝饮食集团旗下，经过入口的水族箱和酒柜，迎面的是以红色为主调的用餐区，红色吊灯、深木色陈设为餐厅添上了中国韵味。这儿提供各式受欢迎的广东菜肴，从经典的咕噜肉至令人垂涎的花胶炆鹅掌，包罗万有，更少不了由香港厨师主理的广式点心。亦设二至十人套餐。

SINGAPORE
新加坡

TEL.+65 6732 2232
Great World City, #02-05A/6, 1 Kim Seng Promenade, River Valley
金声河畔道1号世界城#02-05A/6
www.imperialtreasure.com

♿ ⟷ 🅿 ☏🍴

SINGAPORE
新加坡

TEL.+65 6732 7838

Paragon Shopping Centre, #05-42/45, 290 Orchard Road, Orchard

乌节路290号百利宫#05-42/45

www.imperialtreasure.com

IMPERIAL TREASURE SUPER PEKING DUCK (PARAGON)
御宝至尊烤鸭店（百利宫）

Considered the jewel in the crown of the Imperial Treasure group, this restaurant specialises in Peking duck and is divided into three rooms, with the main one largely kept for bigger parties. After roasting, the whole duck is sliced at the table with a fair degree of ceremony; the skin is crisp and the meat succulent. Don't ignore other dishes like poached Soou Hock fish fillet with chicken broth, and crispy rice roll for lunchtime dim sum. Booking is a must.

所属集团旗下餐厅中的珍宝，享负盛名的京式烤鸭选用马来西亚鸭种，厨师會即席将完整的鸭片成薄片，隆重得像宗教仪式！烤鸭皮薄香脆、肉质鲜美，难怪成为镇店菜式！烤鸭以外，浓鸡汤浸津白笋殻球亦同样用心制作，所使用鸡汤以老鸡熬制八小时而成，且每日鲜制两次。繁忙时间建议订座。六人或以上可点选套餐。

MAJESTIC
大华

Reopened in 2018 at this location, the airy dining room sits under a glass roof and overlooks a garden. The food combines modern techniques with time honoured traditions and is exquisite in both taste and appearance. Try their dim sum, Hor-fun noodles made in house or Hakka ginger wine chicken soup with no water added. Business diners can opt for items in individual servings. Reservations a week ahead are recommended.

从酒店迁至现址的时尚商业大楼内，独特的环境设计和人工庭园让餐厅倍添时尚气息，在此品尝传统却口味新鲜的精致粤菜实是赏心乐事。推介原汁原味、不加水制作的客家姜酒鸡煲，厨师手拉河粉也值得一试。选址商业区，餐厅为菜单作特别安排，不少菜式以一人为上菜单位，方便商务客人。座位不多，建议提前一星期预订。

SINGAPORE
新加坡

TEL.+65 6250 1988

Marina One, The Heart (East Tower)
#04-01, 5 Straits View, Marina Square
海峡林景5号滨海盛景 The Heart #04-01

www.restaurantmajestic.com

ASIA 亚洲

Majestic

MAN FU YUAN
满福苑

A comfortable space, professional service and a fairly priced menu combine to make this Cantonese restaurant, within the InterContinental hotel, a good choice. The kitchen brigade has remained unchanged for a long time and is celebrated for a number of its dishes: double-boiled black chicken soup with fish maw and conch; tea-smoked duck; and roasted suckling pig, for which two day's notice is required – the seafood is also always a popular choice.

厨房团队由经验丰富的香港主厨领导。花胶海螺炖鸡汤、樟茶鸭、烧乳猪及海鲜都是这儿无人不晓的名菜。装潢方面，以木地板、米色墙身、中式摆设及柔和的灯光作布置，感觉舒适自然。价钱相宜，侍应的服务态度也专业，是一间不错的粤菜馆。

SINGAPORE
新加坡

TEL.+65 6825 1008
InterContinental Hotel, Level 2, 80 Middle Road, Bugis
密驼路80号洲际酒店2层
manfuyuan.sg

Man Fu Yuan

🍴🍽

PEONY JADE (KEPPEL)
玉河畔（吉宝）

You don't need to be a member of Keppel Club to visit its Cantonese restaurant. In a large room with beams, dark wood panelling and hanging red lanterns, you'll find food that's full of flavour, carefully prepared and reasonably priced. On the dim sum lunch menu, the hot and sour meat dumplings and pan-fried radish cake with preserved meat are a must. On the main menu try the deep-fried prawns with creamy egg yolk along with some Sichuan dishes.

SINGAPORE
新加坡

TEL.+65 6276 9138
Keppel Club, M level, 10 Bukit Chermin Road, Keppel Bay
武吉慈明路10号岌巴具乐部M层
www.peonyjade.com

🍽 🍴 🅿 🍷

香软奶皇流沙包、京川饺子、腊味煎萝卜糕、鲜虾腐皮卷、脆皮明虾角、京都排骨……全是光听名字便会令你口角垂涎的经典粤式美食，也是主厨的看家菜。木梁天花、红红的灯笼、绘有国画的中式屏风和红木中式家具摆设，带有浓浓中国风的设计，让你不论在味觉还是视觉上都能饱尝传统的味道。

Peony Jade

🍴

SHANG PALACE
香宫

This comfortable and graceful Cantonese restaurant within the Shangri-La hotel is designed to give the impression that you're 'dining in a Chinese garden'. Cantonese cuisine is the mainstay of the menu but there are also Shanghainese influences. Chef Mok, who joined the kitchen crew in 2017, reinvented the menu by adding some innovative twists. However, the traditional dishes are just as good.

获誉为狮城最高级食府之一，餐厅以花卉和中式庭园为装潢主题，散发浓浓的东方韵味。厨房团队由新加入的主厨莫师傅所带领，不但将海派元素揉合到粤菜菜式中，更加入了一些配搭新颖的广东菜式，然而传统口味亦不容错过。服务周到，餐酒选择丰富，甚至包括中国的黄酒和烈酒。

ASIA 亚洲

SINGAPORE
新加坡

TEL.+65 6213 4398

Shangri-La Hotel, Lobby Level, 22 Orange Grove Road, Orchard

柑林路22号香格里拉酒店大堂楼层

www.shangri-la.com/singapore

🎗 ♿ 🏛 🥢 🅿 🍴

AUDREY & MOK PHOTOGRAPHY/Shang Palace

TUNGLOK HEEN
同乐轩

Judicious lighting, dark wood and tones of red combine to give this contemporary Chinese restaurant at Sentosa's Hotel Michael a slick and stylish feel. In among the traditional Chinese dishes are others boasting surprisingly creative combinations, and presentation is always quite striking. Don't miss the double-boiled superior fish bone soup with fish maw; the roast duck; or the coconut jelly with crispy black forbidden rice.

设计时尚的餐室，予人轻松的感觉。供应的菜式不限于传统中菜，独特的创作与烹调风格和精致的卖相，带给食客新鲜感。不可不尝的除了鱼骨浓汤炖花胶外，还有伦敦烤鸭。甜品系列的椰皇脆紫米椰雪花同样出色。要在圣淘沙内找一家有素质的中菜馆，这儿绝对是其中一家值得考虑的。

SINGAPORE
新加坡

TEL.+65 6884 7888
Hotel Michael, #02-142/143, Resorts World Sentosa, 26 Sentosa Gateway, Sentosa
圣淘沙桥门26号圣淘沙名胜世界迈克尔酒店 #02-142/143
www.tunglokheen.com

ASIA 亚洲

Tunglok Heen

TUNGLOK SIGNATURES (CLARKE QUAY)
同乐经典（克拉码头）

Good ingredients and authentic flavours make this Chinese restaurant a worthy choice if you're seeking sustenance in The Central shopping mall. It is one of four branches in Singapore and you can choose between Cantonese, Shanghainese and Sichuan dishes. Specialities include charcoal-grilled honey pork shoulder, and crisp fried Sakura chicken. It's a big, busy and keenly run restaurant, with outside tables that provide good views of Clarke Quay.

SINGAPORE
新加坡

TEL.+65 6336 6022

The Central, #02-88, 6 Eu Tong Sen Street, Clarke Quay

余东旋街6号The Central#02-88

www.tungloksignatures.com

位处克拉码头地铁站之上，晚膳时段可选择户外座位，饱览码头的醉人景致。餐厅有四家分店，其餐牌和供应的菜式一样绚烂夺目，在这里可尝到广东菜、上海菜和四川菜。上乘的食材、传统的风味融合厨师的时尚风格，带来讨人欢心的菜式，例如炭烧蜜汁猪肩肉、脆皮樱花鸡等等。服务殷勤友善。

Tunglok Signatures

WAH LOK
华乐

A loyal clientele have made this comfortable, classically decorated Cantonese restaurant their own. The chef was born in Guangzhou but really developed his culinary skills and honed his craft in Hong Kong. His Cantonese dishes range from banquet delicacies like abalone and bird's nest soup to seafood dishes such as steamed fish. There are also Guangdong roast meats, claypot dishes and home-style dishes like steamed minced pork with salted fish.

华乐是本地很受欢迎的粤菜馆之一，设于酒店主楼座内，设计富现代感的餐室非特别豪华却讨人欢喜。原籍广州的大厨于香港学艺，餐单提供种类繁多的广东菜，无论是宴席菜式如鲍鱼燕窝，海鲜菜式如蒸海鱼，以至别具风味的煲仔菜、广东烧味和家常菜式，都让你品尝到正宗的粤菜口味。

SINGAPORE
新加坡

TEL.+65 6311 8188

Carlton Hotel, 76 Bras Basah Road, City Hall
勿拉士峇沙路76号卡尔登酒店
www.carltonhotel.sg

ASIA
亚洲

Wah Lok

SINGAPORE
新加坡

TEL.+65 6506 6887

**The St. Regis Hotel, Level 1U,
29 Tanglin Road, Orchard**

东陵路29号瑞吉酒店1-U层

www.yantingrestaurant.com

YAN TING
宴庭

Since the name translates as 'Imperial Court'
it's no real surprise this is a very comfortable
room, ideal for impressing visitors and friends.
The extensive Cantonese menu focuses on
traditional dishes, with specialities like braised
supreme sea cucumber with corn broth; prawn
and pumpkin soup; wok-fried lobster with XO
sauce; and braised oxtail in a claypot. The
small alcoves are popular with those wanting
a more intimate dining experience.

和煦的色调、时尚典雅的布置和宽敞的扶手椅,都
令这餐厅成为浪漫晚餐和商务午餐的上佳之选。
这里提供经典的广东菜肴,餐单选择丰富,驰名菜
式包括小米扣辽参、金粟烧汁煎带子、南瓜浓汤烩
虾球、头抽煎羊肚菌鸡脯、红酒烩牛尾煲和宴庭
XO酱龙虾炒饭。

Yan Ting

ASIA 亚洲

BANGKOK
曼谷

Sanyod • SeanPavonePhoto/iStock

SANYOD (SATHON-BANG RAK)

This tiny noodle shop tucked away in a small alley has attracted a loyal fan base for over 50 years with its tasty Thai-Cantonese fare. Regulars come for the chargrilled roast duck marinated with a secret sauce from the shop's founder. Egg noodles get a boost in egg content for extra fluffiness. There are four branches in town and this one is the original shop that seats only 25 people but it has extended to a restaurant on the opposite side of the street.

这家小小的面馆隐藏在小巷里已有五十多年，以泰粤美食吸引到一批忠实的支持者，他们常来品尝以创办人秘制酱汁腌制的炭烧鸭；而鸡蛋面条在制作时特别多加了蛋液，使口感相当松软。餐厅在城里有四家分店，这家是原店，只能容纳二十五人，现已在对面街道上加开了一个铺面。

BANGKOK
曼谷

TEL.+66 2 236 3905
89 Soi Charat Wiang, Bang Rak
www.sanyodrestaurant.com

P ⓒ|| s

AH YAT ABALONE FORUM (RAMADA PLAZA MENAM RIVERSIDE HOTEL)

BANGKOK
曼谷

TEL.+66 2 291 7781

2F, Ramada Plaza Menam Riverside Hotel, Charoen Krung Road, Bang Kho Laem

Traditional Cantonese delights, like suckling pig and stir-fried shrimp, dominate the menu, but the real magic is in Chef Yeung's secret recipe for braised abalone and off-menu seasonal dishes that regular patrons know to request. Cooking techniques are by the book, and deliveries from Singapore ensure that prawns, grouper, lobster, and razor clams are fresh. Private rooms make this a fun affair for large groups.

传统粤式美食如乳猪和炒虾球是菜单上的主角,然而真正富有魔力的菜肴,是杨主厨以秘制配方炮制的红烧鲍鱼,以及不在菜单之上、但老顾客都懂得点的时令菜式。烹调方式谨遵传统,虾、石斑鱼、龙虾和蛏子都是从新加坡新鲜运到。私人厢房适合大型团体举办聚会。

Michelin

CHEF MAN (SATHON)

Hong Kong-born chef Man Wai Yi has earned a reputation in town for his Cantonese cuisine and consistently good quality dim sum. The Peking duck is legendary, but you'll need to call and order one day in advance; other standout dishes include the Chef Man-style wagyu short ribs. Chef Man is particularly keen on producing an authentic "home-style" cuisine – which is no real surprise as each station in his kitchen is manned by chefs from Hong Kong.

凭着出色的粤菜和出品稳定的巧手点心，香港出生的厨师文师傅在城里赢得了声誉。要一尝镇店菜式北京烤鸭的话，紧记提前一天电话预订。招牌菜文式和牛小排骨是主厨以自家研制的方法烹调，风格独特。厨房里各个步骤皆由来自香港的厨师负责，这正好解释了主厨何以特别热衷于烹调正宗的家常菜式。

BANGKOK
曼谷

TEL.+66 2 212 3741
3F, Eastin Grand Sathorn, 33/1
Sathon Tai Road, Sathon
www.chefmangroup.com

ASIA 亚洲

CHEF MAN

⫶⃝

LEE KITCHEN

Bangkok never runs short of choices in Chinese food and this is one of those with a long history. Founded in 1989, it has served thousands of happy customers who return for their homemade dim sum and other signature dishes such as Mr Lee Duck, seabass with egg noodle soup and sautéed crab claw in spicy sauce. The owner-chef reflects his Chao Zhou descent in the menu and only the freshest ingredients make it to the kitchen.

BANGKOK
曼谷

TEL.+66 2 213 1018
26/37-38 Chan Tat Mai Road, Sathon
www.leekitchenthai.com

⟷ ⃝⫶

曼谷从来不缺中国菜,而李酒店是其中一家历史悠久的餐厅,于1989年创立,一再光临的客人数以千计,吸引他们的美食包括自家制点心、李氏招牌鸭、鲈鱼汤面和铁板蟹钳。从菜单中可以看出东主兼大厨祖籍潮州,且只会使用最新鲜的食材烹调。

MEI JIANG

Overlooking the lush gardens of The Peninsula Hotel on the banks of the Chao Phraya River, Mei Jiang – which means beautiful river – is an elegant Cantonese restaurant. Classic Chinese delights are prepared by an experienced chef from Hong Kong, and the staff are consummate professionals. Dim sum is a highlight and the "Health" set menu satisfies both the stomach and body and is a speciality of the chef.

TEL.+66 2 020 2888

GF, The Peninsula Hotel, 333 Charoennakorn Road, Khlong San

www.peninsula.com

湄江是一家高雅的粤菜餐厅，位置正好可以俯瞰昭拍耶河畔半岛酒店茂密的园林。来自香港的厨师拥有丰富的经验，他与极其专业的团队合力精心制作出中国的经典美食。点心是餐厅的重点，而大厨特别设计的"健康"套餐则既能满足味觉，又有益身体。

Mei Jiang

xiao zhou/iStock

EUROPE
欧洲

BELGIUM
比利时

TANG'S PALACE

A Chinese restaurant located in the town for over 20 years. 'Tikpan' speciality (cooking on tables in cast iron dishes). Renovated setting. Walls adorned with photos of Asian cities.

富豪在城內经营超过二十年，专门做"铁板烧"（在桌上用铁板烹制菜肴）。室内重新装修过，墙壁上挂着一些亚洲城市的照片。

AALST
阿尔斯特

TEL.+32 53 78 77 77
Korte Zoutstraat 51, 9300, Oost-Vlaanderen

www.tangspalace.be

A/C

BIJ LAM & YIN

Lam & Yin is definitely not a run-of-the-mill Asian restaurant. Don't expect paper lanterns or a menu as long as the Great Wall of China! This is the place for delicate, subtle Cantonese cuisine, depicted by fresh, original flavours and a quest for authenticity before all else. Genuine saké is served in the Gang Bei.

燕林绝对不是一家平凡的亚洲餐厅,不要以为会见到纸灯笼或是长度宛如中国长城的菜单!在这里可以品尝到可口又精致的粤菜,原汁原味,入口清新,追求粤菜的正宗口味。餐厅提供正品的清酒。

ANTWERPEN
安特卫普

TEL.+32 3 232 88 38
Reynderstraat 17, 2000, Antwerpen
lam-en-yin.be

5 FLAVORS MMEI

The most well-known and the most obvious can sometimes surprise – and this restaurant is a perfect example. The chef pays homage to Chinese tradition with fresh and sometimes surprising preparations, which put paid to many prejudices regarding the cuisine of his place of birth. The dim sum are to die for!

具名气的餐厅有时也会带来惊喜，而这儿正是绝佳例子。主厨采用新鲜的食材和令人意想不到的方式入馔，以向中国传统致敬，也摒除了部分人对主厨出生地菜式的偏见。餐厅的点心水准尤其超卓！

ANTWERPEN
安特卫普

TEL.+32 3 281 30 37
Volkstraat 37, 2000, Antwerpen

EUROPE 欧洲 • BELGIUM 比利时

Kanawa_Studio/iStock

CUICHINE

Two childhood friends, both sons of restaurant owners, created Cuichine with the idea of serving dishes they used to eat at home. Their Cantonese recipes are well prepared from fresh produce and without fussy frills. Even better, the à la carte menu is well priced and the lunch menu unbeatable.

两个儿时玩伴各自都是餐馆老板的儿子，他俩一起创办了家膳，供应以前在家里吃的菜式。餐厅的广东菜都是用新鲜食材烹制，卖相不会过于花巧。更难得的是单点菜单价格合理，午餐菜单更是无可匹敌。

ANTWERPEN
安特卫普

TEL.+32 3 289 92 45
Draakstraat 13, 2018, Antwerpen
www.cuichine.be

LIANG'S GARDEN

A stalwart of Chinese cuisine in the city! A spacious restaurant where the authentic menu covers specialities from Canton (dim sum), Peking (duck) and Sichuan (fondue).

这家餐厅是城内中国菜的中坚分子！餐厅面积宽敞，提供的是正宗中国菜，包括来自广东的点心、北京的烤鸭和四川的火锅菜式。

ANTWERPEN
安特卫普

TEL.+32 3 237 22 22

Generaal Lemanstraat 54, 2018, Antwerpen

www.liangsgarden.eu

AC ⟷

JODOIGNE
若杜瓦涅

TEL.+32 10 88 17 28

chaussée de Hannut 8, 1370, Brabant Wallon

SCHUN MING

An authentic Chinese restaurant located on the corner of a busy road. The à la carte offers a large number of traditional Chinese dishes which are all equally delicious. Numerous set menus are also available.

这家正宗的中式餐厅就位于城里一条繁忙街道的拐角处。单点菜单上有大量传统中式菜肴，各类菜式均美味可口。面对着琳琅满目的单点菜单难以决定的话，也有众多套餐可供选择。

LE TEMPLE DU GOÛT

This "temple of flavours" offers a relaxed culinary journey through China and Thailand through classic dishes revisited with a contemporary flair. Dishes are prepared on the spot at the sushi bar at the front of the restaurant.

在品味轩吃饭，让人尤如进入了"味道的神殿"，在轻松的环境下经历中泰两地的美食之旅，更能细味以现代手法重新演绎的经典菜肴。餐厅前方的寿司吧就是美食出场的位置。

LIEGE
列日

TEL.+32 4 239 28 85
route du Condroz 457, 4031, Liège
www.letempledugout.be

EUROPE 欧洲 • BELGIUM 比利时

CHEZ CHEN

Despite its location in the heart of Belgium, this restaurant run by the Chen family (the mother and daughter are in the dining room, the father in the kitchen) takes guests on a journey back to China thanks to the Asian touches in its contemporary and stylish decor, but above all the refinement and flavours of its cuisine.

NAMUR
那慕尔

TEL.+32 81 74 74 41
chaussée de Dinant 873, 5100, Namur
www.chezchen.be

这家餐厅由家族经营，母亲和女儿招待客人，父亲负责掌厨。尽管餐厅位于比利时中部，仍能让食客经历一趟中国之旅。这除了要归功于其带有亚洲风情的时尚装潢设计，最重要的还是既精致又风味十足的菜肴。

JARDIN DE PÉKIN

At the "Peking Garden" your tastebuds are transported back to China! Here, (re)discover the very best Chinese recipes (wanton soup, dim sum, Peking duck) to a backdrop of typical decor.

京苑酒楼把你的味蕾带回中国去了！在典型的中式装饰背景前，你将发掘到顶级的中国菜式，包括馄饨汤、点心和北京烤鸭。

WOLUWE-SAINT-PIERRE
沃吕韦 一 圣彼得

TEL.+32 2 770 45 37

Parvis Sainte-Alix 32, 1150, Brussel-Hoofdstad / Bruxelles-Cap

www.lejardindepekin.be/

A/C

FRANCE
法国

SHANG PALACE

The Shang Palace occupies the lower floor of the Shangri-La hotel where it gracefully recreates the decor of a luxury Chinese restaurant with its jade columns, sculpted screens and crystal chandeliers. The menu pays homage to the full flavours and authenticity of Cantonese cuisine.

香宫位于香格里拉酒店低层，餐厅内的玉石柱、雕刻屏风和水晶吊灯营造了优雅豪华的用餐环境。菜单呈献的每一道菜式都是向风味十足且正宗的粤菜致敬。

PARIS
巴黎

TEL.+33 1 53 67 19 92
10 avenue d'Iéna, 75116
www.shangri-la.com

EUROPE 欧洲 • FRANCE 法国

Shang Palace • EHStock/iStock

IMPÉRIAL CHOISY

A Chinese restaurant in the heart of the city's Chinatown frequented by the local Asian community who use it as their regular lunchtime haunt. In a dining room that never empties (non-stop service, perhaps a little too efficient!), enjoy superb Cantonese specialities cheek by jowl with other diners. A truly authentic experience that won't break the bank.

这家餐厅位于巴黎唐人街的中心地带,极受当地亚洲社群欢迎,是不少食客午餐时的固定聚脚点。在那座无虚席的用餐区,服务员殷勤地服务,紧挨着的食客一起享受高素质的广东菜肴,是价格相宜的美食体验。

PARIS
巴黎

TEL.+33 1 45 86 42 40
32 avenue de Choisy, 75013

Impérial Choisy

🍴○

DIEP

Asia is very much to the fore both in the decor (black and red colour scheme, alcoves and carved panels) and on the menu here, which includes specialities from Hong Kong and Canton province, as well as a few Thai and Vietnamese dishes. Fish and seafood take particular pride of place.

这家餐厅无论在室内装潢（黑色和红色色系、壁龛和雕花板），还是菜单设计上，都洋溢着亚洲风情。菜单上包括来自香港和广东的特色菜肴，也有泰国和越南菜式，其中鱼和海鲜是餐厅最引以为傲之作。

PARIS
巴黎

TEL.+33 1 45 63 52 76
55 rue Pierre-Charon, 75008
www.diep.fr

A/C 🖐

GOLFX/iStock

EUROPE 欧洲 • FRANCE 法国

LILI

Opened by the Hong Kong luxury hotel group of the same name, the already famous Peninsula Hotel provides the setting for its restaurant, Lili, named after a famous Chinese singer from the 1920s. In this very theatrical setting, the extensive menu reveals a wide array of Chinese specialities in what is a temple for Chinese cuisine!

莉莉中菜厅位于半岛酒店内,由享负盛名的同名香港酒店集团经营。"莉莉"之名源于1920年代一位著名中国戏曲家,餐厅设计以剧院为主题,置身其中,看着菜单上各式各样的中国菜肴,更令人生出处于中菜殿堂之感!

PARIS
巴黎

TEL.+33 1 58 12 67 50
19 avenue Kléber, 75116
www.peninsula.com/fr/

amarita/iStock

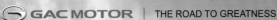

GAC MOTOR | THE ROAD TO GREATNESS

Keep Striving

No one can predict the future,
unless they help to shape it.

From Ordinary to Extraordinary.
Make the Leap

恒　进　取

没有人能预知结果
路只有走过才知道

平凡到伟大

一

步

MER DE CHINE

This restaurant near Place d'Italie specialises in Chao Zhou cuisine from the south of Guangdong province. Enjoy tasty dishes and friendly service to a background of traditional Chinese music.

这家在意大利广场附近的餐厅专门供应潮州菜。食客可以在中国传统背景音乐下品尝美味佳肴，享受宾至如归的服务。

PARIS
巴黎

TEL.+33 1 45 84 22 49

159 rue du Château-des-Rentiers, 75013

A/C

Michelin

¶O

PASSY MANDARIN LA MUETTE

The menu at Passy Mandarin La Muette, which was founded in 1976, focuses very much on continuity. Authenticity is the buzzword in its dishes, which include the great classics of Chinese – but also Thai and Vietnamese – cuisine, prepared and cooked with time-honoured expertise. The decor here firmly embraces its Chinese roots.

陆羽酒家于1976年开业,一如既往地坚持制作正宗菜式,菜单上除了中国经典佳肴外,还有泰国菜和越南菜。从备菜到烹调,各个步骤皆由经验丰富的团队负责。酒家的装潢风格与其中国根源贯彻如一。

PARIS
巴黎

TEL.+33 1 42 88 12 18
6 rue Bois-le-Vent, 75016
www.restaurant-passy-mandarin.fr

TAOKAN – ST-GERMAIN

In this attractive restaurant in the heart of St-Germain des Prés, savour Chinese and, in particular, Cantonese specialities such as dim sum, steamed fish, duck breast with honey, and caramelised sliced chicken. With its beautiful presentation and top-notch ingredients, this restaurant is a true ambassador for Chinese cuisine!

在这家位于圣日耳曼德佩区中心的餐厅品尝中国菜实在令人向往,其广东菜餚特别出色,例如点心、蒸鱼、蜜汁鸭胸和焦糖鸡片等。凭借其精美的摆盘和一流的食材,这家餐厅堪称中华美食大使!

PARIS
巴黎

TEL.+33 1 42 84 18 36
8 rue du Sabot, 75006
www.taokan.fr

EUROPE 欧洲 • FRANCE 法国

🍴○

TAOKAN – ST-HONORÉ

Tao means "the way" and Kan means to "care for". As such, TaoKan is a restaurant that pays tribute to Cantonese food and flavours with the occasional Taiwanese twist. Here, savour dishes such as grilled Peking ravioli and steamed cod with julienne of ginger and a white tea sauce (Bai cha xue yu). A real treat!

TaoKan是一家推崇粤菜的餐厅，菜式偶尔揉合台湾元素。在这里品尝香煎锅贴和姜丝蒸鳕鱼配白茶酱（白茶鳕鱼）等菜肴，确实是一大享受！

PARIS
巴黎

TEL.+33 1 42 61 97 88
1 rue Mont-Thabor, 75001
www.taokan.fr

♿ 🆎 ↔ 🍷

HaizhanZheng/iStock

EUROPE 欧洲 • FRANCE 法国

GERMANY
德国

LONG MARCH CANTEEN

Currently one of "the" places to eat, Long March Canteen offers a dimly lit interior, informal service and a kitchen open to the diners' gaze. The menu features Cantonese fare in the form of a variety of dim sum and dumpling dishes. Wide selection of wines, spirits, cocktails and tall drinks.

长征食堂灯光昏暗,服务不会让人感到拘谨,开放式的厨房可让食客观看里面情况。食堂提供以各式点心和饺子为主打的粤菜,也有多种葡萄酒、烈酒、鸡尾酒和长饮可供选择。

BERLIN
柏林

TEL.+49 178 8849599
Wrangelstr. 20, 10997, Kreuzberg
www.longmarchcanteen.com

EUROPE 欧洲 • **GERMANY** 德国

FRANKFURT
法兰克福

TEL.+49 69 91399050
Konrad-Adenauer-Str. 7, 60313,
Frankfurt am Main
https://sansan-restaurant.de/

SAN SAN

San san offers excellent and authentic cuisine from various Chinese provinces, including dim sum from Guangzhou and beef from Sichuan, in a modern, East-Asian style interior. Alternatively, you can try something a little more traditional in Shanghai Suite.

餐厅提供来自中国各省的优质正宗菜式,包括广式的点心和四川的水煮牛肉。现代化的室内装潢带有东亚风格,您也可以选择在更具传统特色的上海套间里用餐。

zhanglianxun/Fotosearch LBRF/age fotostock

NI HAO

At Ni Hao fans of Chinese cuisine can learn a little more about its four major cooking styles – Canton, Sichuan, Shanghai and Peking – in authentic style. Try the tasty sounding traditional four-course Peking duck menu.

在"你好"，喜欢中国菜的食客可以更加了解中国四个菜系——粤菜、川菜、沪菜和京菜的正宗风味。不妨点选美味的传统北京烤鸭四道菜套餐。

HAMBURG
汉堡

TEL.+49 40 6520888
Wandsbeker Zollstr. 25, 22041,
Wandsbek
www.ni-hao.de

EUROPE 欧洲 · GERMANY 德国

IRELAND
爱尔兰

CHINA SICHUAN

A smart interior is well-matched by creative menus, where Irish produce features in tasty Cantonese classics and some Sichuan specialities. It was established in 1979 and is now run by the third generation of the family.

时髦的室内设计与富创意的菜单显得相得益彰，经典粤菜和四川特色菜采用爱尔兰食材炮制而成。餐厅始创于1979年，现在由家族的第三代经营。

DUBLIN
都柏林

TEL.+353 1 293 5100
The Forum, Ballymoss Rd., D18, Sandyford
www.china-sichuan.ie

ITALY
意大利

KANTON RESTAURANT

Il Kanton has opened a new world to Italian diners unfamiliar with authentic Chinese cuisine. Here, the flavours of the East can be enjoyed in refined dishes which include a mix of traditional recipes and more contemporary fare. To make the most of the delicious options on offer, make sure you ask the waiters for recommendations.

Kanton为不熟悉正宗中国菜的意大利食客开辟了新的世界。在这里，精致的东方菜肴揉合传统与现代风味。如果想尝尽是日美食，谨记请服务员为您推介。

BERGAMO
贝加莫

TEL.+39 02 9096 2671
Via Antonio Gramsci 17, 24042, Capriate San Gervasio
www.kantonrestaurant.it

☲ ᕤ AC

EUROPE 欧洲 • ITALY 意大利

FLORENCE
佛罗伦萨

TEL.+39 055 284331
Via de' Neri 37/r, 50122
www.dimsumrestaurant.it

Ⓐ Ⓒ

🍴○

DIM SUM

This Chinese restaurant is very popular with locals and for good reason. The menu focuses on small portions of fish and meat (dim sum, hence the restaurant's name) accompanied by an excellent selection of teas.

这家中餐厅非常受当地人欢迎，原因毋庸置疑。菜单一如餐厅名字，专门供应点心，搭配精选茗茶。

BA ASIAN MOOD

Ba Asian Mood is run by a family with lots of experience in the restaurant business – and it shows. The elegant dining room is illuminated by subtle lighting, while the typically Chinese cuisine is carefully prepared using top-quality ingredients.

Ba Asian Mood由拥有丰富餐饮业经验的家族经营——并表现得名副其实。典雅的餐室灯光微暗，具代表性的中国菜则采用了顶级食材精心烹制而成。

MILAN
米兰

TEL.+39 02 469 3206
Via R. Sanzio 22 ang. Via Carlo Ravizza 10, 20123
www.ba-restaurant.com

EUROPE 欧洲 • ITALY 意大利

FoodCollection/Photononstop

MILAN
米兰

TEL.+39 02 341308
Via Castelvetro 16/18, 20154
www.bon-wei.it

 ♿ AC

🍴〇

BON WEI

There is no fusion cuisine at this restaurant, simply a choice of specialities made from fresh produce and top-quality ingredients. Served in dark, modern and elegant dining rooms, the dishes come from the many different regions of China.

这家餐厅没有供应混合菜，只提供以新鲜农产品和顶级食材炮制的美食。安坐在灯光柔暗、时尚而优雅的用餐区，您可以品尝到来自中国不同地区的菜式。

CSP_sierpniowka/ Fotosearch LBRF /age fotostock

DIM SUM

In rooms full of decorative detail, this restaurant introduces its guests to the small dishes which characterise the culinary traditions of Canton and southern China. A truly authentic Chinese dining experience.

在装饰细致的房间里，餐厅为客人带来广州和中国南方的传统点心，烹饪富传统特色，无疑是一次正宗中国菜的体验。

MILAN
米兰

TEL.+39 02 2952 2821
Via Nino Bixio 29, 20123
www.dim-sum.it

AK ⟷

GONG

At Gong, Guglielmo and Keisuke delight their guests with their constantly evolving menu which features Italian and Japanese cuisine, as well as Chinese specialities, internationally influenced dishes and plenty of other tempting delicacies.

在Gong，Guglielmo和Keisuke不断改良菜单，以满足客人需求。菜单上除了意大利菜和日本料理，还有中国特色菜、国际风味菜式和很多其他诱人的美味佳肴。

MILAN
米兰

TEL.+39 02 7602 3873
Corso Concordia 8, 20123
www.gongmilano.it

GREEN T.

Owner Yan introduces tea lovers to the "Tao of Tea" (an introduction and tasting of this ancient beverage) in this original restaurant situated on four floors of a building not far from the Pantheon. Asian cuisine takes pride of place on the menu.

在这幢离万神殿不远的四层楼房里，店主Yan让品茶爱好者体验"茶道"（介绍和品尝这种历史悠久的饮料）。亚洲美食是菜单上的重要角色。

ROME
罗马

TEL.+39 06 679 8628
Via del Piè di Marmo 28, 00186
www.green-tea.it

AK ⬚

EUROPE 欧洲 • ITALY 意大利

Green T.

NETHERLANDS
荷兰

🍴

DYNASTY

A pleasant, long-standing restaurant featuring cuisine from around Asia. The trendy, exotic décor is warm and colourful. There's a lovely terrace at the back and service is attentive.

这家令人感到舒坦的老店供应亚洲各地美食。时尚的室内装潢散发异国情调,温暖又色彩缤纷。餐厅后方有一个漂亮的露台,服务体贴周到。

AMSTERDAM
阿姆斯特丹

TEL.+31 20 626 8400
Reguliersdwarsstraat 30, 1017 BM,
Noord-Holland
www.fer.nl

🛖 A/C 🍽

EUROPE 欧洲 • NETHERLANDS 荷兰

DE MANGERIE

De Mangerie is a great Chinese restaurant where your taste buds are taken on a tour across all of China's provinces. Well-known favourites like Peking duck and tiger prawns are authentically flavoured but offer a little bit more punch than most.

De Mangerie是一家很棒的中餐厅，她让您的味蕾周游在中国各個省份的菜式中。北京烤鸭和虎虾等著名美食味道正宗，比其他餐厅的更多了一份感染力。

HILVERSUM
希尔弗瑟姆

TEL.+31 35 672 0784

**Diependaalselaan 490, 1215 KM,
Noord-Holland**

www.demangerie.nl

AC

ROYAL MANDARIN

An elegant restaurant where Chinese cuisine takes on a European twist. Guests will recognise the characteristic flavours, presented in combination with regional ingredients and paired with excellent wines.

这家高雅的餐厅供应的中国菜揉合欧洲风格，采用当地食材炮制，并配以优质餐酒，菜式独特的风味让食客一试难忘。

HILVERSUM
希尔弗瑟姆

TEL.+31 35 640 0801

Emmastraat 9, 1211 NE, Noord-Holland

www.royalmandarin.nl

Royal Mandarin

LEIDEN
莱顿

TEL.+31 71 579 0216
Alexandrine Tinneplein 96, 2331 PP,
Zuid-Holland
www.alexanderleiden.nl

🅰🄲 ⇔

🍴

ALEXANDER

From Sichuan to Beijing, from pure authenticity to contemporary sophistication, Alexander introduces guests to different facets of Chinese cuisine. The Asian interior of this large establishment is plain and simple but the flavours are lavish. Whether you opt for an authentic, refined or fusion dish, it is guaranteed to taste good.

从四川到北京，从正宗传统到现代的精致，皇子酒楼都能为食客带来中国菜的不同面貌。这家宽广餐厅的亚洲风室内装潢简单朴素，然而菜式的味道却是丰富讲究。无论您选择正宗的、精致的还是混合菜肴，都能保证吃得津津有味。

Michelin

¶○

WEN-CHOW

Situated directly opposite the station, this restaurant serves authentic Chinese cuisine, as the number of loyal Chinese regulars testifies.

这家餐厅位于车站的正对面，供应的中国菜肴口味地道，看看有多少华裔老顾客光顾就知道名副其实了。

MAASTRICHT
马斯特里赫特

TEL.+31 43 321 4540
Spoorweglaan 5, 6221 BS, Limburg
www.wen-chow.nl

⌂ A/C

EUROPE 欧洲 • NETHERLANDS 荷兰

NUNSPEET
宁斯佩特

TEL.+31 341 252 829
Harderwijkerweg 85, 8071 EN,
Gelderland
www.ni-hao.nl

NI HAO

This modern restaurant has an intimate Eastern feel. The chef combines traditional and contemporary flavours in his dishes (specialities from Sichuan, Guangdong, Beijing and Wenzhou), which present a modern take on authentic Chinese cuisine.

这家时髦的餐厅带有宜人的东方风情。厨师烹调的川菜、粤菜、京菜和温州菜将传统和现代的风味结合，在正宗中国菜上呈现出现代感。

Ni Hao

ASIAN GLORIES

Asian Glories offers authentic, high quality Chinese cuisine, which focuses on the culinary traditions of Canton and Sichuan. Specialities on the menu include Peking duck and the delicious dim sum, a type of Oriental dumpling that is served either boiled or fried.

东方之珠提供正宗而高品质的中国菜，专注于广东和四川的传统烹调方式。菜单上的特色菜包括北京烤鸭，还有水煮和香煎均可的东方饺子。

ROTTERDAM
鹿特丹

TEL.+31 10 411 7107
Leeuwenstraat 15, 3011 AL, Zuid-Holland
www.asianglories.nl

A/C

EUROPE 欧洲 • NETHERLANDS 荷兰

SOESTERBERG
苏斯特贝赫

TEL.+31 346 351 423
Rademakerstraat 2, 3769 BD, Utrecht
www.orientalswan.nl

THE ORIENTAL SWAN

A comfortable Asian restaurant located on the main road in Soesterberg. Here, Cantonese flavours reign supreme, although the menu also features some Thai dishes. 'Rijsttafels' (rice tables) and set menus are also available.

这家舒适的餐厅位于苏斯特贝赫市的主要大道上，虽然菜单供应泰国菜、东南亚特色菜式Rijsttafels和套餐，然而最受食客欢迎的美食始终是粤菜。

HaizhanZheng/iStock

EUROPE 欧洲 • NETHERLANDS 荷兰

NORWAY
挪威

DINNER

An intimate restaurant on the central square, close to the National Theatre. A black frosted glass façade masks a smart split-level interior. The kitchen focuses on Sichuan cuisine, with some artfully presented dim sum at lunch.

这家舒适宜人的餐厅位于中央广场，邻近国家剧院。室内巧妙地运用了黑色磨砂玻璃去处理复式错层。餐厅以供应四川菜为主，午市提供制作精致的点心。

OSLO
奥斯陆

TEL.+47 23 10 04 66
Stortingsgata 22, 0161
www.dinner.no

AC ⬚

SWITZERLAND
瑞士

TSÉ FUNG

Cantonese – and Chinese cooking in general – can count on Frank Xu to act as its gastronomic ambassador here. His culinary creations are authentic and delicious in equal measure, meticulously prepared with the very best ingredients. His desserts, in particular, will live long in the memory. Pleasant view of the garden and lake.

大厨Frank Xu炮制的粤菜和中式菜肴都有很高的水平，令他毫无疑问地成为中菜的美食大使。他的出品正宗而可口，会为每一道菜精心准备最优质的食材，甜点特别令人难以忘怀。餐厅旁的花园和湖泊风光宜人，为美食之旅平添自然色彩。

GENEVA
日内瓦

TEL.+41 22 959 59 59

Route de Lausanne 301, 1293, Bellevue

www.tsefung.ch

EUROPE 欧洲 • SWITZERLAND 瑞士

UNITED KINGDOM
英国

A. WONG

A modern Chinese restaurant with a buzzy ground floor and a sexy basement. The talented eponymous chef reinvents classic Cantonese dishes using creative, modern techniques; retaining the essence of a dish, whilst adding an impressive lightness and intensity of flavour. Service is keen, as are the prices.

这家时髦的中餐厅有热闹的地面层和迷人的地库。餐厅以主厨命名,他运用创意和现代技巧重新演绎经典粤菜,在保留原有精粹的同时,亦加添了令人印象深刻的轻盈感和香浓的味道。服务热情周到,与价格成正比。

LONDON
伦敦

TEL.+44 20 7828 8931
70 Wilton Rd, SW1V 1DE, Victoria
www.awong.co.uk

🚇 AC

EUROPE 欧洲 • UNITED KINGDOM 英国

HAKKASAN HANWAY PLACE

LONDON
伦敦

TEL.+44 20 7927 7000
8 Hanway Pl., W1T 1HD, Bloomsbury
www.hakkasan.com

There are now Hakkasans all over the world but this was the original. It has the sensual looks, air of exclusivity and glamorous atmosphere synonymous with the 'brand'. The exquisite Cantonese dishes are prepared with care and consistency by the large kitchen team; lunch dim sum is a highlight.

餐厅分店遍布世界各地,而这家正是首家店子。餐厅有着动人的外观,独特气息和华丽氛围令人目眩,正好与品牌匹配。精美讲究的粤式菜肴由庞大的厨房团队精心准备,出品水准稳定;午市点心是一大特色。

HaizhanZheng/iStock

HAKKASAN MAYFAIR

If coming for lunchtime dim sum then sit on the ground floor; for dinner ask for a table in the moodily lit and altogether sexier basement. The Cantonese cuisine uses top quality produce and can be delicate one minute; robust the next. There are also specialities specific to this branch.

如果午市来尝尝点心，可以选择地面层；来吃晚餐的话，就要求在那神秘又迷人的地库就座吧。餐厅采用最上乘的食材烹调粤菜，手法多变，喜爱清新别致或浓烈醇厚的皆不乏选择。此店更设有独家菜式。

LONDON
伦敦

TEL.+44 20 7907 1888
17 Bruton St, W1J 6QB, Mayfair
www.hakkasan.com

EUROPE 欧洲 • UNITED KINGDOM 英国

KAI

Both the owner and his long-standing chef Alex Chow are Malaysian and, while the cooking features dishes from several provinces in China, it is the southern region of Nanyang which is closest to their hearts. The unashamedly glitzy look of the restaurant is as eclectic as the food and the service team are switched on and fully conversant with the menu.

东主和主厨周师傅都来自马来西亚,菜单上固然有源自中国不同省份的菜式,然而最拿手的始终要数南洋南部地区的菜肴。室内装潢一如食物般光芒四射,服务团队殷勤周到且对餐牌了若指掌。

LONDON
伦敦

TEL.+44 20 7493 8988

65 South Audley St, W1K 2QU, Mayfair

www.kaimayfair.co.uk

Kai Mayfair

YAUATCHA SOHO

2019 is its 15th birthday but it still manages to feel fresh and contemporary, with its bright ground floor and moody basement, featuring low banquettes, an aquarium bar and a star-lit ceiling. Dishes are colourful with strong flavours and excellent texture contrasts; dim sum is the highlight – try the venison puff.

餐厅将在2019年踏入十五周年，门面却依然光鲜而充满现代感。一楼灯火通明，地库气氛神秘，特色是低矮的长条椅、水族箱酒吧和星光闪闪的天花板。菜肴色彩丰富，味道浓郁，质感对比鲜明；点心尤其出色，推介鹿肉酥。

LONDON
伦敦

TEL.+44 20 7494 8888
15 Broadwick St, W1F 0DL, Soho
www.yauatcha.com

EUROPE 欧洲 • UNITED KINGDOM 英国

jason lowe ltd/Yauatcha Soho

327

¶IO

DUCK & RICE

Something a little different – a converted pub with a Chinese kitchen – originally set up by Alan Yau. Beer and snacks are the thing on the ground floor; upstairs, with its booths and fireplaces, is for Chinese favourites and comforting classics.

这家有点不一样的餐厅—— 一家带有中式厨房的酒吧，由丘德威（Alan　Yau）创办。地面层供应啤酒和小食，设有厢座和火炉的楼上则有中华美食和经典菜式。

LONDON
伦敦

TEL.+44 20 3327 7888
90 Berwick St, WIF 0QB, Soho
www.theduckandrice.com

AC

ROYAL CHINA CLUB

Service is fast-paced and to the point, which is understandable considering how busy this restaurant always is. The large menu offers something for everyone and the lunchtime dim sum is very good; at dinner try their more unusual Cantonese dishes.

服务员节奏勤快，正因为餐厅经常座无虚席。选择多样的菜单上罗列了切合大众口味的菜式，午膳点心值得推介，晚饭时间到来可尝尝其与别不同的广东菜肴。

LONDON
伦敦

TEL.+44 20 7486 3898
40-42 Baker St, W1U 7AJ, Marylebone
www.royalchinagroup.co.uk

aspas/iStock

TEL.+44 20 8749 9978

**58 Shepherd's Bush Grn, W12 8QE,
Shepherds Bush**

www.shikumen.co.uk

♿ A/C

SHIKUMEN

Impressive homemade dim sum at lunch and excellent Peking duck are the standouts at this unexpectedly sleek Cantonese restaurant in an otherwise undistinguished part of Shepherd's Bush.

没想到在牧羊人丛林区内不起眼的地段，能在这家整洁的餐厅里品尝到令人印象深刻的粤菜，午市自制点心和极其美味的北京烤鸭都是其代表作。

GMVozd/iStock

YAUATCHA CITY

A more corporate version of the stylish Soho original, with a couple of bars and a terrace at both ends. All the dim sum greatest hits are on the menu but the chefs have some work to match the high standard found in Broadwick Street.

相比苏豪区风格时尚的总店，这家分店显得较商业化，餐厅两端都设有数个酒吧和一个露台。最受食客欢迎的点心应有尽有，但厨师还更精益求精，以贯彻Broadwick街的高水準。

LONDON
伦敦

TEL.+44 20 3817 9880

Broadgate Circle, EC2M 2QS, City of London

www.yauatcha.com

EUROPE 欧洲 • UNITED KINGDOM 英国

madisonwi/iStock

USA
美国

CHICAGO
芝加哥

JADE COURT

Its location is a bit out of the way (unless you're a student at UIC) and its digs may leave much to be desired, but Jade Court is certainly worth the trek. The same father-daughter team that once owned Phoenix in nearby Chinatown now runs this Cantonese kitchen. The large carte features an impressive variety of dim sum and casseroles; while blazing-hot woks turn out black bean and garlic stir-fries as well as sizzling hot plates that arrive brimming with seafood. And although most dishes come as small portions, they can still feed a group at a fraction of the price. Think of honey-glazed barbecue pork that glistens with just the right amount of fat; pan-fried noodles layered with tender beef strips; or Chinese broccoli boasting that perfect crunch.

USA 美国

翠华阁的位置有点偏僻（除非你是UIC的学生），但依然值得一试。父女档的店东曾经营唐人街附近的万濠，现在这家餐厅供应各式各样的粤菜，丰富的菜单上有多样点心和煲仔菜，也有热腾腾的小炒，或铁板海鲜等铁板菜式。虽然大多数的菜肴分量小，但价格相宜。令人回味的，还有肥瘦适中的蜜汁叉烧、干炒牛河或爽脆的炒芥兰。

CHICAGO
芝加哥

TEL. +1 312-929-4828

626 S. Racine Ave., 60607, Pilsen, Illinois

www.jadecourtchicago.com

335

MINGHIN

位于华埠广场地面层，交通便利。宽敞的用餐区以木格板分隔出多种场合的座位间隔，从休闲聚餐到宴会圆桌，以至特别装备的火锅桌都有。点心在平日也大受欢迎，食客可按图点选，不用等待点心车。在众多选择中，最受欢迎的是饱满多汁的虾饺；内有猪肉和冬菇的腊味萝卜糕煎得香脆幼滑，而松软的蒸马拉糕是比较特别的甜点。

Conveniently situated on the ground level of Chinatown Square, MingHin is a stylish standby that draws a diverse crowd to the neighborhood. Spacious dining rooms separated by wooden lattice panels offer seating for a number of occasions, from casual booths and large banquet-style rounds to specially outfitted tables for hot pots. Dim sum is a popular choice even on weekdays, with diners making selections from photographic menus rather than waiting for a passing cart. Among the numerous options, juicy har gao, stuffed with plump seasoned shrimp, always hits the spot. Pan-fried turnip cakes are simultaneously crispy and creamy, studded with bits of pork and mushroom. Fluffy and subtly sweet Malay steamed egg cake is a rare find for dessert.

CHICAGO
芝加哥

TEL.+1 312-808-1999

2168 S. Archer Ave., 60616,
Chinatown & South, Illinois

www.minghincuisine.com

PHOENIX

Dim sum lovers get the best of both worlds at Phoenix, a comfortable room that boasts a grand view of the Chicago skyline. Here, stacks of bamboo baskets are wheeled to tables on signature silver trolleys for a classic dim sum experience-yet each diner's selection is cooked to order for truly fresh and steaming-hot bites. The proof is in the soft and poppable shrimp-and-chive dumplings and the fluffy white buns stuffed with chunks of barbecue pork. Those looking for larger portions will appreciate the meandering menu, which also boasts Hong Kong-style stir-fry and clay pot dishes alongside Americanized Chinese classics. Fillets of steamed sea bass swim in soy oil on a large oval platter, sprinkled with a touch of slivered scallion to brighten the delicately flaky fish.

TEL. +1 312-328-0848

2131 S. Archer Ave., 60616,
Chinatown & South, Illinois

www.chinatownphoenix.com

点心爱好者在万濠能两全其美，既能在舒适的环境欣赏芝加哥天际线的壮丽景色，也可以享受经典点心。银色手推车上是一堆堆的竹笼点心，有饱满的韭菜虾饺和满载馅料的松软叉烧包，现叫现蒸，确保新鲜美味。长长的菜单中也有各式各样的小菜，包括香港风味的小炒、煲仔菜和美式中国经典菜肴，例如以生抽和葱花调味的蒸鲈鱼片。

USA 美国

NEW YORK
纽约

CONGEE VILLAGE

From the edge of Chinatown comes Congee Village, with its neon-etched sign that shines bright at night. Coveted for its fantastic cooking (check the front window for a slew of accolades), the menu also has a Cantonese focus. Service is basic and the décor kitschy at best, but it's clean, tidy, and tons of fun. This soothing namesake porridge comes in myriad forms – ladled into a clay pot with bits of crispy roasted duck skin, or mingled with pork liver and white fish to form an intense and rich flavor combination. Pair it with dunkable sticks of puffy deep-fried Chinese crullers for a satisfying contrast in texture. Less adventurous palates may deviate into such solid standards as sautéed short ribs and sweet onions tossed in a smoky black pepper sauce.

位处唐人街边陲，粥之家的霓虹灯招牌在晚上格外显眼，一如令人垂涎的佳肴（前窗展示了大量荣誉证书），菜单以粤菜为主，装饰略嫌土气，却是整洁有趣。同是粥品都可有无数组合形式——加块酥脆的烤鸭皮；或是混合猪肝和鱼片，令瓦煲里的粥分外绵稠浓郁；用油条伴着吃，质感对比让人满足。铁板黑椒牛仔骨等小菜的水准有保证。

NEW YORK
纽约

TEL.+1 212-941-1818

100 Allen St., 10002, Manhattan, Lower East Side, New York

www.congeevillagerestaurants.com

2018 Michelin Guide • cmart7327/iStock

USA 美国

DIM SUM GO GO

餐厅长期满座的原因毋庸置疑：这里的粤菜和点心与偏远的皇后区无比正宗的食店里的素质一样好，而且这店接受订位，加上点餐是由服务员下单，确保点心新鲜。建议避开周末繁忙时段，因需要拼桌，服务也较混乱。食品价格比同类餐厅稍高，却是物有所值，例如米纸甜虾卷配老抽、豌豆叶饺子、味道浓郁的鸭肉饺子和令人难以抗拒的叉烧酥。

This wildly popular joint is still packed to the gills most days, and for good reason: the Cantonese fare and dim sum served here is as good as the food you'll find in those super-authentic places in far-flung Queens. Even better, they take reservations – and dim sum orders are taken by the staff, thereby ensuring that the food stays fresh. However, guests should avoid shared tables during the weekend rush as service can verge on chaotic. If the price seems a bit higher than its competitors, you'll find it's worth it for dishes like sweet shrimp, rolled in rice paper and laced with dark soy sauce. Plump snow pea leaf dumplings are spiked with vibrant ginger, garlic, and may be tailed by rich duck dumplings or an irresistibly flaky roast pork pie.

NEW YORK
纽约

TEL.+1 212-732-0797

5 East Broadway, 10038, Manhattan, Chinatown & Little Italy, New York

2018 Michelin Guide

EAST HARBOR SEAFOOD PALACE

Dim sum is a well-orchestrated dance at this boisterous hall, where small crowds wait for a spot at one of the large round tables for an indulgent weekend brunch. Steaming carts roll by and waiters ferry trays briskly into the red dining room with shiny gold accents. Service is quick but helpful; the constant clatter of chopsticks and rollicking groups are part of the fun. Eyes can guide the ordering when it comes to the dim sum carts, stocked with authentically prepared bites. Try the plump shrimp siu mai followed by rice noodles wrapped around crunchy whole shrimp and doused in a sweet-salty soy sauce. Snappy, stir-fried green beans are addictively crunchy. Don't miss the Singapore mei fun, a mound of vermicelli noodles with shrimp, pork, and scallions.

TEL.+1 718-765-0098

714-726 65th St., 11220, Brooklyn, Sunset Park & Brighton Beach, New York

人群等着尽情享用周末早午拼餐，服务员以手推车和托盘在闪金配大红的用餐区来回传菜，服务敏捷，面面俱到。筷子铿锵的碰撞声与食客的欢笑声相映成趣。看到手推车上的传统点心就随心点选，建议品尝饱满多汁的虾烧卖，还有浇上酱油的爽弹鲜虾肠粉和爽脆的炒青豆，也别错过有虾仁、猪肉和香葱的星洲炒米。

USA 美国

这家占地数层的老店，是少数面积
如此宽广的粤菜餐馆，让一批批热
气腾腾的点心车周游。服务有效率，
建议早点抵埗坐近厨房位置以享受
更多点心选择，食物也更温热。到处
推介美食如叉烧包或皮蛋瘦肉粥的
服务员热心助人。本地人和游客熙来
攘往，环境也适合有小孩的家庭，受
欢迎程度一如可口的鲜虾豆苗饺、
烧卖和鲜虾肠粉。

NEW YORK
纽约

TEL.+1 212-941-0911

**18 East Broadway, 10002, Manhattan,
Chinatown & Little Italy, New York**

www.goldenunicornrestaurant.com

GOLDEN UNICORN

This age-old dim sum parlor, spread over
many floors in an office building, is one of
the few Cantonese spots that actually has the
space and volume to necessitate its parade of
steaming carts brimming with treats. While
Golden Unicorn's system is very efficient
and part of the spectacle, arrive early to nab
a seat by the kitchen for better variety and
hotter items. A helpful brigade of suited men
and women roam the space to offer the likes
of exquisitely soft roast pork buns, or congee
with preserved egg and shredded pork.
Buzzing with locals and visitors, it is also a
favorite among families who appreciate the
kid-friendly scene as much as the delectable,
steamed pea shoot and shrimp dumplings,
pork siu mai, and rice rolls stuffed with shrimp.

2018 Michelin Guide

GREAT N.Y. NOODLETOWN

When heading to Great N.Y. Noodletown, invite plenty of dining companions to share those heaping plates of roasted meats and rice and noodle soups served at this bargain favorite. Locals stream in until the 4:00 A.M. closing bell for their great Cantonese fare – food is clearly the focus here, over the brusque service and unfussy atmosphere. Guests' gazes quickly pass over the imitation wooden chairs to rest on the crispy skin of suckling pig and ducks hanging in the window. These dishes are huge, so forgo the rice and opt instead for deliciously chewy noodles and barbecue meats. Incredible shrimp wontons, so delicate and thin, and the complex, homemade e-fu noodles demonstrate technique and quality to a standout level that is rarely rivaled.

光临此餐厅，记得呼朋唤友以分享分量大且价格便宜的烤肉、米饭和汤面。出色的粤菜吸引本地食客光顾至凌晨四点。服务和氛围不拘小节，食客可以清楚看到挂在橱窗上的乳猪和烧鸭有多香脆。菜肴分量大，可以放弃米饭，改要美味弹牙的面条和烧肉。精致的虾馄饨外皮薄得令人惊叹，还有自制的伊面，制作技巧和质量都出色得无与伦比。

NEW YORK
纽约

TEL.+1 212-349-0923

28 Bowery, 10013, Manhattan, Chinatown & Little Italy, New York

这家粤式餐厅神秘又精致，大门后是一条灯光昏暗的长走廊，通向巨型的用餐区，钴蓝色玻璃、卡拉拉大理石和镜子为偌大的空间营造了亲密感。令人垂涎的菜肴有茉莉花茶熏鸡和蜜糖豆炒蟹肉带子、竹蒸笼带子飞鱼籽烧卖、皇帝蟹肠粉和松露烤鸭包。点心套餐价格相宜，在這以奢华为基调的餐厅，这实在是一个可以让人尽情放纵的惊喜。

NEW YORK
纽约

TEL.+1 212-776-1818

311 W. 43rd St., 10036, Manhattan,
Midtown West, New York

www.hakkasan.com

ⅱ○

HAKKASAN

If this sensual and sophisticated lair doesn't come to mind when you crave quality Cantonese cooking, it's high time you added it to the list. Behind its front door lies a long, moodily-lit corridor that leads to a massive dining room, which, thanks to cobalt-blue glass, Carrara marble, and mirrors, feels intimate despite its size. The equally elegant menu underscores mouthwatering dishes like jasmine tea-smoked chicken and stir-fried sugar pea pods with crabmeat and scallops; or bamboo steamers full of scallop siu mai topped with tobiko, King crab noodle rolls, as well as truffle and roasted duck bao. The prix-fixe dim sum, a wallet-friendly delight that synchs perfectly with Hakkasan's luxe tenor, is yet another decadent surprise.

USA 美国

SAN FRANCISCO
旧金山

KOI PALACE

Long regarded as one of the Bay Area's best spots for dim sum, Koi Palace continues to earn its serious waits (guaranteed on weekends, and common at weekday lunch). The dining room is a step up from its competition, with shallow koi ponds weaving between tables, high ceilings, and huge tables to accommodate the Chinese-American families celebrating big occasions. They come to share plates of perfectly lacquered, smoky-salty roasted suckling pig or sticky rice noodle rolls encasing plump shrimp, sesame oil, and minced ginger. Not far behind, find lotus leaves stuffed with glutinous rice, dried scallop, and roast pork, as well as big pots of jasmine tea. Save room for desserts like the fluffy almond cream steamed buns and flaky, caramelized custard tarts.

鲤鱼门长期被誉为湾区最佳点心餐厅之一，等候入座的食客人山人海（周末如是，平日午市常见）。用餐区有锦鲤池和高耸的天花，也有足够容纳华裔家庭欢聚的大桌子，分享烧得光亮如漆入口带烟熏味的乳猪、鲜虾肠粉，以及放满了糯米、瑶柱及烧肉的糯米鸡，配上大壶香片茶。记得预留肚皮给雪山杏汁包和酥皮葡挞等甜品。

DALY CITY
戴利城

TEL.+1 650-992-9000

365 Gellert Blvd., 94015, Peninsula, California

www.koipalace.com

MILLBRAE
米尔布雷

TEL.+1 650-692-6666

51 Millbrae Ave., 94030, Peninsula, California

www.mayflower-seafood.com

一代接一代的点心忠实支持者经常为了一尝叉烧包而光顾。甫坐下，服务员就推着点心车来推介数之不尽的美食：脆皮烧腩仔、即叫即做的鲜虾韭菜果，还有精致的素饺和一流的雪山流沙包。晚市较平静，主力推介用鲜活食材做的粤式海鲜。早来的顾客会有较佳的点心选择（并避免周末的轮候情况）。位于市中心确保停车位充足，熟练的车场员工服务到位。

HONG KONG FLOWER LOUNGE

Generations of dim sum diehards have patronized this palace of pork buns, where a small army of servers will surround you with carts from the moment you take your seat. They bear innumerable delights: rich barbecue pork belly with crispy skin, pan-fried pork-and-chive wontons steamed to order and doused in oyster sauce, delicate vegetable dumplings, and a best-in-class baked egg custard bun. Evenings are a bit more sedate, emphasizing Cantonese seafood straight from the on-site tanks. As with all dim sum spots, the early bird gets the best selection (and avoids the non-negligible weekend waits). Thankfully, the super-central Millbrae location, towering over El Camino Real, boasts plenty of parking-and a machine-like staff that knows how to pack them in.

MISTER JIU'S

Chef/owner Brandon Jew has brought some of the sparkle back to Chinatown with this contemporary treasure, which puts a modern Californian spin on the Cantonese classics that once made this neighborhood a national dining destination. Impressively, the chef also makes all his Chinese pantry staples in-house, like the oyster sauce that coats a stir-fry of smoked tofu with long beans, tripe and tendon.

The menu is full of these clever touches, from the tomalley that adds depth to a rich Dungeness crab egg custard to the "tentacles" of fried fennel that echo the texture of salt-and-pepper squid.

Set in a longtime banquet hall, Mister Jiu's is bright and airy, with dramatic brass lotus chandeliers overhead.

大厨兼店东Brandon将现代加州风格融入经典粤菜，更自家制作所有中式食材，如在长豆角牛肚牛筋炒烟熏豆腐中所用的蚝油。菜单上满是巧妙设计，蟹膏令黄金蟹蛋羹倍添滋味，触须状的茴香与椒盐鱿鱼互相呼应。餐厅明亮开扬，缀以夸张的黄铜莲花吊灯。

SAN FRANCISCO
旧金山

TEL.+1 415-857-9688

28 Waverly Pl., 94108, Nob Hill, California

www.misterjius.com

HONG KONG LOUNGE II

餐厅外有夺目的粉色外墙，里面有湾区最好的午市点心。没有手推车而是直接用点心纸下单，众多选择中推介松化的焗叉烧餐包、蒜蓉大豆苗和无与伦比的鸡蛋挞。供应上等茶叶，素食菜单也相当丰富，难怪周末早上来候座的食客挤得水泄不通。虽然与Geary Boulevard的Hong Kong Lounge名字相似，但两家没有附属关系，食物也不太一样。

SAN FRANCISCO
旧金山

TEL.+1 415-668-8802

3300 Geary Blvd., 94118, Marina, California

www.hongkonglounge2.com

If the bland peach exterior of this restaurant doesn't entice you, trust that a juicy treasure lies beneath: some of the Bay's best dim sum offered at lunch. Skipping the carts for a made-to-order approach, the sizable menu groans with winners, including flaky, buttery baked pork buns, sautéed pea shoots delectably flavored with garlic, and one of the best egg custard tarts you're ever likely to taste - even if you've visited Hong Kong. Throw in above-average tea options and a sizable vegetarian menu, and it's no wonder that this tiny gem draws legendary waits on weekend mornings. Just don't turn tail and head for the other Hong Kong Lounge further down Geary-despite their names, the two aren't affiliated, and the food isn't quite the same.

LAI HONG LOUNGE

This windowless dim sum lounge looks small from the outside, but there's room for over 100 diners inside its cherry-red dining room – with dozens more hopefuls lined up on the street outside. The largely Chinese crowd attests to the authenticity of the food, which ranges from steamed pork buns and taro dumplings to chicken feet with peanuts. (If you're hoping to skip out on the wait, go at dinner instead of lunch, or call for takeout). Smiling servers roll carts featuring no end of tasty options, so you'll have to make some hard choices. Favorites include gingery wonton soup, full of soft and savory little dumplings; enormous rice noodle rolls stuffed with ground beef and aromatic herbs; and crispy, golden pan-fried tofu with a silky interior.

TEL.+1 415-397-2290

1416 Powell St., 94133, North Beach, California

www.lhklounge.com

这家没有窗户的点心馆看来很小，其实用餐区能容纳超过一百位食客。门外有数十人轮候入座，顾客大多是中国人，可见食物正宗，从叉烧包、芋角，到花生凤爪皆有（不想排队的建议晚间光临或叫外卖）。笑容可掬的服务员推着点心车穿梭，种类包罗万有，让人难以选择。大受欢迎的点心有姜味馄饨汤、香茜牛肉肠粉和外脆内软的黄金豆腐粒。

USA 美国

TEL.+1 415-580-3001

845 Market St., 94102, SoMa,
California

www.tastemychina.com

M.Y. CHINA

要证明甄能煮？就到这位大厨兼
PBS节目主持人的餐厅试试。位处
购物中心的穹顶下，餐厅放满了高
级的中式家具和古董，坐满了逛累了
的人，站满了欣赏手拉面和抛锅技术
的饕客。菜单主打中国地方菜，野猪
刀剪面带嚼劲，叉烧包內满是带甜
烟熏味的猪肉，辣椒螃蟹是时令佳
肴。记得要有策略地点菜，最后还得
吃那完美的澳门葡式蛋塔。

Need proof that Yan Can Cook? Just snag
a table at the famed PBS chef's elegant
restaurant. Housed under the dome of the
Westfield San Francisco Centre shopping
mall, M.Y. China is a dark, sultry space full
of posh Chinese furniture, antiques, and
dramatic lighting. Shopping-weary patrons
fill the dining room, whereas chowhounds
hit the exhibition counter to watch the staff
masterfully hand-pull noodles and toss
woks. The menu reads like an ode to regional
Chinese cuisine, spanning chewy scissor-cut
noodles with wild boar, fluffy bao stuffed with
sweet and smoky barbecue pork, and, when
it's in season, delectable pepper-dusted whole
crab. Be sure to order strategically, as you'll
want room for the flaky, buttery, creamy, and
outright superb Macanese egg tarts.

YANK SING

With a higher price tag than the average Chinatown joint, Yank Sing is arguably the place in town for dim sum. The upscale setting boasts reasonable prices, but the zigzagging carts can get hectic. While peak hours entail a wait, one can be assured of quality and abundant variety from these carts rolling out the kitchen. The signature Peking duck with its crispy lacquered skin and fluffy buns makes for a memorable treat, not unlike the deliciously sweet and salty char siu bao. Of course, dumplings here are the true highlight, and range from fragrant pork xiao long bao, to paper-thin har gao concealing chunks of shrimp. Don't see favorites like the flaky egg custard tarts? Just ask the cheerful staff, who'll radio the kitchen for help via headsets.

城内吃点心的好地方，收费与高档的环境成正比。服务员来回推着点心车，里面是素质高而种类繁多的点心。招牌菜北京烤鸭有油亮的脆皮，伴着松软的包子一起吃，味道实在难忘；甜中带咸的叉烧包同样滋味。真正的拿手之作是各种饺子，如芳香的猪肉小笼包和皮薄馅多的虾饺。找不到松化蛋塔等热卖点心的话，可问问乐于助人的服务员。

SAN FRANCISCO
旧金山

TEL.+1 415-781-1111
101 Spear St., 94105, SoMa, California
www.yanksing.com

INDEX OF RESTAURANTS

餐厅列表

STARRED RESTAURANTS 星级餐厅

🏵️🏵️🏵️

🏵️🏵️

🏵️

BIB GOURMANDS 必比登美食推介

PLATE 米其林餐盘

CREDITS:

MICHELIN TRAVEL PARTNER
Société par actions simplifiée au capital de 15 044 940 €
27 Cours de L'Île Seguin – 92100 Boulogne Billancourt (France)
R.C.S. Nanterre 433 677 721

© 2018 Michelin Travel Partner – All rights reserved
Legal deposit: 09-2018
Printed in China: 09-2018

Typesetting: Nord Compo, Villeneuve d'Ascq (France)
Printing – Binding: Book Partners China (China)